Autism and Criminal Justice

This collection presents a summary of current knowledge regarding autistic suspects, defendants and offenders in the criminal justice system of England and Wales. The volume examines the interaction between each stage of the criminal justice process and autistic individuals accused or convicted of crime, considering the problems, strengths and possibilities for improving the system to better accommodate the needs of this vulnerable category of neurodiverse individuals. By explicating the core issues in this important but disparate area of study in a single place, the collection facilitates understanding of and engagement with knowledge for a wider audience of relevant stakeholders, including criminal justice practitioners, policy makers, academics and clinicians. It also incorporates key recommendations for improvement, thereby clarifying the urgent need for substantive change in policies and practices. The ultimate goal is to both improve the treatment and experience of autistic people subjected to criminal justice processes; and produce fairer, more appropriate systemic outcomes. While focused on the criminal justice system of England and Wales, the work will be valuable for researchers and policy makers working in similar systems, as well as those interested in neurodiversity more generally.

Tom Smith is an Associate Professor in Law and a Head of the Global Security, Crime and Justice research group within the College of Business and Law, University of the West of England (UWE), Bristol, UK. His research interests include remand, disclosure of evidence in criminal proceedings, criminal defence lawyers, criminal legal aid, court reporting and open justice, and neurodivergence within the criminal justice system. He has published widely on these and related subjects. He has undertaken various research activities with NGOs, charities and government bodies, including working on cross-jurisdictional projects related to criminal defence and a pretrial detention reform project in China; delivering training for the Judicial College and College of Policing on disclosure; and giving evidence to the Victorian Royal Commission into the Management of Police Informants and various House of Commons Select Committee inquiries. He is the founder and joint coordinator of the Neurodivergence in Criminal Justice Network (NICJN), a research and knowledge exchange group seeking to promote evidence-led practice in criminal justice processes involving neurodivergent individuals, which brings together expertise from academia, practice and the community.

Routledge Contemporary Issues in Criminal Justice and Procedure

Series Editor **Ed Johnston** is an Associate Professor of Criminal Justice and Procedure at the University of Northampton, UK.

Efficiency and Bureaucratisation of Criminal Justice
Global Trends
Edited by Ed Johnston and Anna Pivaty

Murder, Wrongful Conviction and the Law
An International Comparative Analysis
Edited by Jon Robins

A History of Victims of Crime
How they Reclaimed their Rights
Stephen J. Strauss-Walsh

Vulnerability, the Accused, and the Criminal Justice System
Multijurisdictional Perspectives
Edited by Roxanna Dehaghani, Samantha Fairclough and Lore Mergaerts

Covid-19 and Criminal Justice
Impact and Legacy in England and Wales
Edited by Ed Johnston

Witness Protection and Criminal Justice in Africa
Nigeria in International Perspective
Suzzie Onyeka Oyakhire

Autism and Criminal Justice
The Experience of Suspects, Defendants and Offenders in England and Wales
Edited by Tom Smith

Robotics, AI and Criminal Law
Crimes against Robots
Kamil Mamak

See more at https://www.routledge.com/Routledge-Research-in-Legal-History/book-series/CONTEMPCJP

Autism and Criminal Justice

The Experience of Suspects, Defendants and Offenders in England and Wales

Edited by Tom Smith

Routledge
Taylor & Francis Group

LONDON AND NEW YORK

First published 2023
by Routledge
4 Park Square, Milton Park, Abingdon, Oxon OX14 4RN

and by Routledge
605 Third Avenue, New York, NY 10158

Routledge is an imprint of the Taylor & Francis Group, an informa business

© 2023 selection and editorial matter, Tom Smith; individual chapters, the contributors

British Library Cataloguing-in-Publication Data
A catalogue record for this book is available from the British Library

Library of Congress Cataloging-in-Publication Data
Names: Smith, Tom (Thomas) (Lecturer in law), editor.
Title: Autism and criminal justice: the experience of suspects, defendants and offenders in England and Wales/edited by Tom Smith.
Description: Abingdon, Oxon; New York, NY: Routledge, 2023. | Series: Routledge contemporary issues in criminal justice and procedure | Includes bibliographical references and index. |
Identifiers: LCCN 2022061668 | ISBN 9781032164861 (hardback) | ISBN 9781032164878 (paperback) | ISBN 9781032164861 (ebook)
Subjects: LCSH: Offenders with mental disabilities–England. | Offenders with mental disabilities–Wales. | Special needs offenders–England. | Special needs offenders–Wales. | Discrimination in criminal justice administration–England. | Discrimination in criminal justice administration–Wales. | Autistic people–Legal status, laws, etc.–England. | Autistic people–Legal status, laws, etc.–Wales.
Classification: LCC HV6133 .A87 2023 | DDC 364.3/8–dc23/eng/20230105
LC record available at https://lccn.loc.gov/2022061668

ISBN: 978-1-032-16486-1 (hbk)
ISBN: 978-1-032-16487-8 (pbk)
ISBN: 978-1-003-24877-4 (ebk)

DOI: 10.4324/9781003248774

Typeset in Times New Roman
by Deanta Global Publishing Services, Chennai, India

Contents

Acknowledgements   ix
List of Contributors   x
List of Abbreviations   xiv
List of Figures   xvi
Table of Cases   xvii
Table of Legislation   xviii

Introduction   1
TOM SMITH

1 'Street' Policing and Autism: Perceptions and Preconceptions
   of Police Officers When Interacting with Autistic Suspects in
   the Community   10
   SHIRLEY REVELEY AND IAIN DICKIE

2 Autistic Suspects in Police Custody: Issues Affecting the
   Effectiveness and Fairness of Police Interviews   29
   CLARE ALLELY AND DAVID MURPHY

3 Autistic Defendants in Court: Perceptions and Support for
   Accessing Justice   45
   CLARE ALLELY, EDDIE CHAPLIN, JODY SALTER, JANE McCARTHY AND
   FELICITY GERRY

4 Autism in Prisons: An Overview of Experiences of Custody
   and Implications for Custodial Rehabilitation for
   Autistic Prisoners   62
   LUKE P VINTER AND GAYLE DILLON

Conclusion 82

TOM SMITH

Bibliography 93
Further Recommended Reading 108
Index 109

Acknowledgements

I would like to thank a number of key figures in the creation of the collection. First, an enormous thank you to the contributing authors, not only for your stimulating and high quality work, but for your patience during the gestation of this book. Second, I am deeply grateful to Dr Ed Johnston (Routledge series editor) and Alison Kirk (Routledge commissioning editor) for your guidance and support, as well as your faith in this collection and its topic material. Finally, the biggest thank you goes to my family, Kirsty and Alex—not only for your support and love, but for fundamentally inspiring my drive to bring this collection to fruition.

Tom Smith

Contributors

Clare Allely is a Professor of Forensic Psychology at the University of Salford in Manchester, England, and is an affiliate member of the Gillberg Neuropsychiatry Centre at Gothenburg University, Sweden. Allely holds a PhD in psychology from the University of Manchester and graduated with an MA (hons.) in psychology from the University of Glasgow, an MRes in psychological research methods from the University of Strathclyde and an MSc in forensic psychology from Glasgow Caledonian University. Allely is also an honorary research fellow in the College of Medical, Veterinary and Life Sciences at the University of Glasgow. She is also an associate of the Children and Young People's Centre for Justice (CYCJ) at the University of Strathclyde. Allely is a research leader on the subject of autism and criminal justice, having examined issues arising at multiple stages of the system including in police custody, courts and prisons. She is widely published in peer-reviewed journals and had her book *Autism Spectrum Disorder in the Criminal Justice System* published by Routledge in 2022. Allely also acts as an expert witness in criminal cases and has contributed to the evidence base used in the courts on psychology and legal issues through her published work.

Eddie Chaplin is a Professor of Mental Health in Neurodevelopmental Conditions at the Institute of Health and Social Care, London South Bank University. He originally studied mental health interventions, completing his MSc at Middlesex University, followed by a PhD in health services research at the Institute of Psychiatry, Psychology & Neuroscience at King's College London. His main research interests include identification and understanding neurodevelopmental conditions in the criminal justice system, an overrepresented and largely unrecognised group with high rates of need who are often unable to access treatment or diversion to more suitable services. He is interested in co-produced research around self-help and peer mentoring strategies around improving mental health. He is currently head of the Scientific Committee for the European Association of Mental Health in Intellectual Disability and the editor for the journal *Advances in Autism*. He has published extensively in peer-reviewed journals and authored several books and training packs.

Iain Dickie is an Independent Researcher and Counsellor at Improving Access to Psychological Therapies (IAPT) North Cumbria Integrated Care Trust, and was previously a social researcher and lecturer in Counselling and Psychotherapy at the University of Cumbria. In the past few years, he has been actively involved with a research project looking into the experience of people on the autism spectrum within the criminal justice system; the focus of his research has centred on perceptual barriers to communication between autistic and neurotypical individuals. He has also previously undertaken training in counselling and psychotherapy as well as criminology and sociology. Dickie and colleagues presented key findings from their autism-specific research project at the 17th International Conference on Offenders with an Intellectual and/or Developmental Disability, organised by the National Autistic Society. In addition, he has co-authored papers presenting initial findings from interviews with criminal justice service staff within Cumbria in the *Journal of Applied Psychology and Social Science*.

Gayle Dillon is a Principal Lecturer in Psychology at Nottingham Trent University; a member of the Sexual Offences, Crime and Misconduct Research Unit (SOCAMRU) at the university; and teaches in the MSc in Applied Child Psychology. Her teaching and research interests cover developmental and forensic psychology, with a focus on children and adults with additional support needs in educational and forensic settings. She has worked extensively in school settings with a particular focus on autism. She has worked on a variety research projects, delivered papers at national and international conferences, and published articles in journals, including the *International Journal of Developmental Disabilities* and the *British Journal of Psychology*.

Felicity Gerry is an international King's Counsel at Libertas Chambers, London, and Crockett Chambers, Melbourne; Honorary Professor at Salford University in the School of Health and Society; and Professor of Legal Practice at Deakin University, Australia. Her legal practice largely involves defending in serious and complex criminal trials and appeals, often with an international element. She has extensive court experience in significant legal challenges, including leading the successful appeal in

R v Jogee (2016) in the UK Supreme Court. She is a high-profile legal expert, sought out by broadcasters for media commentary and presentation on international legal issues, particularly relating to international crimes, terrorism and homicide, and corporate responsibility for human rights abuses. She is commonly called to comment upon issues from her teaching and research on women and law, technology and law, and reforming justice systems. Additionally, her research focuses on autism and criminal law, female genital mutilation law, and child rights. She also made successful submissions to governments which have led to changes in the law on modern slavery, female genital mutilation and reproductive rights.

Jane McCarthy is a Consultant Psychiatrist in Intellectual Disability with the East London NHS Foundation Trust; and Associate Professor, University of Auckland. She has worked for over 20 years as a senior psychiatrist in specialist services for adolescents and adults with intellectual disabilities and autism. From 2009 to 2010, McCarthy acted as clinical advisor for adults with autism at the Department of Health in England supporting development and delivery of the national strategy for adults with autism. McCarthy's key research interests include the outcomes of psychiatric disorders in people with neurodevelopmental disorders. She has published more than 60 peer-reviewed research papers and chapters. In 2012 she was elected chair of the International Association for Scientific Study of Intellectual and Developmental Disabilities (IASSIDD) Challenging Behaviour & Mental Health Special Interest Research Group, which is the largest global research network in this field of research. She is vice chair of the Psychiatry of Intellectual Disability Faculty, Royal College of Psychiatrists, UK.

David Murphy is a Neuropsychologist, West London NHS Trust, based at Broadmoor, high-security psychiatric hospital. Murphy has more than 24 years of experience of working in a range of forensic settings. As a practicing chartered forensic and consultant clinical neuropsychologist, Murphy has particular expertise in the assessment and management of high-risk individuals with autism. Murphy is also an active researcher examining various aspects of autism in forensic settings with a number of publications in international peer-reviewed journals, as well as acting as an expert witness for a number of high-profile criminal cases, including within the Crown Courts and at the Court of Appeal.

Shirley Reveley is a Honorary Fellow and Visiting Research Professor, University of Cumbria; and an Emeritus Professor, The Open

University. She holds a PhD in primary health care from Lancaster University, focusing on the role of the nurse practitioner in primary care and has been closely involved in research and development of this advanced nursing role. Reveley has published and presented at many conferences on the topic of autism. More recently, she has been involved in examining how adults with Autism Spectrum Disorder experience contact with criminal justice services.

Jody Salter is a PhD Researcher at the University of Salford. Salter's doctoral thesis investigates whether the presentation of behavioural features integral to Autism Spectrum Disorder (ASD) in the courtroom impacts juror perceptions of credibility, and subsequent decision-making, which may lead to poorer outcomes in the criminal justice system. Salter holds an MSc in clinical neurodevelopmental sciences from King's College London, in which she obtained a distinction. Her master's dissertation was titled 'The effectiveness of interventions for offending behaviours in adults with ASD: a systematic PRISMA review.' She also holds a BSc in psychology with neuroscience from Birkbeck, University of London. Salter's research interests include neurodevelopmental disorders; biological influences on human behaviour and their interaction with the legal system; radicalisation and extremism; and intersectionality in people with ASD.

Luke P Vinter is a Senior Lecturer in Applied Criminology, Department of Law and Social Sciences, University of Derby; and member of the Sexual Offences, Crime and Misconduct Research Unit (SOCAMRU), based at Nottingham Trent University. Coming from an academic background of psychology, law and criminology, Vinter's research has predominantly related to working with autistic individuals in prison settings. Specifically, this has included projects focusing on working with autistic individuals in prison-based interventions to address sexual offending, and supporting autistic individuals serving prison sentences more generally. Vinter has also conducted research relating to supporting other vulnerable prisoner populations, such as older prisoners with dementia.

Abbreviations

AAA	All About Autism
ADHD	attention deficit hyperactivity disorder
ADI-R	Autism Diagnostic Interview-Revised
ADOS-G	Autism Diagnostic Observation Schedule-Generic
APA	American Psychiatric Association
AQ-10	Autism Spectrum Quotient
ASC	Autism Spectrum Condition
ASD	Autism Spectrum Disorder
CJJI	Criminal Justice Joint Inspection
CJS	criminal justice system
CPD	Continuing Professional Development
DHSC	Department of Health and Social Care
DoE	Department of Education
DSM-5	*Diagnostic and Statistical Manual of Mental Disorders, Fifth Edition*
E&W	England and Wales
EHRC	Equality and Human Rights Commission
GCS	Gudjonsson Compliance Scale
GSS 2	Gudjonsson Suggestibility Scale 2
HEE	Health Education England
HMCTS	HM Court and Tribunals Service
HMP	HM Prison
HMYOI	HM Young Offender Institution
ICD-11	*International Classification of Diseases and Related Health Problems, Eleventh Revision*
ID	intellectual disability
L&D	Liaison and Diversion
LEO	law enforcement officer
MHCLG	UK Ministry of Housing, Communities and Local Government
MoJ	UK Ministry of Justice

MORM	multifactor offender readiness model
NAS	National Autistic Society
NDD	neurodevelopmental disorder
NDM	National Decision Model
NDTI	National Development Team for Inclusion
NICE	National Institute for Health and Care Excellence
NPAA	National Police Autism Association
OBP	offender behaviour programme
PACE	Police and Criminal Evidence Act 1984
RBRIs	repetitive behaviours and restricted interests
TEACCH	Treatment and Education of Autistic and related Communication-handicapped Children
ToM	theory of mind
WHO	World Health Organization

Figures

4.1 Medical model view of autism   63
4.2 Social model view of autism   63
4.3 Visualisation of the iceberg analogy   75
4.4 Multifactor offender readiness model (MORM)   78

Table of Cases

R v Dunleavy [2021] EWCA Crim 39
R v Grant-Murray and Henry [2017] EWCA Crim 1228
Sultan v R [2008] EWCA Crim 6

Table of Legislation

Autism Act 2009
Bail Act 1976
Health and Care Act 2022
Human Rights Act 1998
Mental Health Act 1983
Police and Criminal Evidence Act 1984 (PACE) Code C
     revised: Code of practice for the detention, treatment and
     questioning of persons by police officers (2019)
Police Officer Training (Autism Awareness) Bill 2019, HC Bill
     386 (2017–19)
Youth Justice and Criminal Evidence Act 1999

Introduction

Tom Smith

Overview

It is perhaps an understatement to say that, at the time of writing, the criminal justice system (CJS) of England and Wales faces an unprecedented and toxic mix of substantial challenges. There are numerous pressing issues, for example, the large backlog of cases (exacerbated, but not caused, by the COVID-19 pandemic); squeezed funding across the CJS (exemplified by the high-profile dispute over legal aid remuneration for barristers during 2022); and concerns about the use of custody, including a ballooning remand population and reports of extensive, long-term solitary confinement (User Voice and Queen's University Belfast, 2022). In combination, these problems—among many others—genuinely threaten the short- and long-term efficacy of English and Welsh criminal justice.

These challenges are also occurring in a context of rapid transformation of the way we 'do' justice. Examples might include the expanding use of remote court hearings and video link attendance for participants; the increased involvement of complex digital forensic evidence in cases; and the use of artificial intelligence and machine learning in policing. As such, the system and its professionals face both existential threats, which require resolution, and significant changes, which demand swift adaptation. Set amongst this maelstrom of change and challenge is the vital and enduring need to ensure fair processes which protect vulnerable individuals from injustice and trauma as a result of involvement in criminal justice processes. Arguably, in this uncertain context, ensuring effective and equal access to justice for vulnerable individuals is more difficult, and urgent, than ever before.

DOI: 10.4324/9781003248774-1

One such category of vulnerability, and the focus of this collection, is the autistic individual subject to criminal justice processes. Autism[1] is a neurodevelopmental disorder (or, from a social model perspective, difference; see Oliver, 1983; Woods, 2017) which is typically characterised by impairments in social reciprocal interactions and communication, and restricted, repetitive patterns of interests and behaviour (American Psychiatric Association, 2013; see also Allely & Cooper, 2017). It also commonly involves a variety of sensory processing differences, such as hyper-reactivity (increased sensitivity) and hypo-reactivity (reduced sensitivity) to particular sensory stimuli (Crane, Goddard, & Pring, 2009). Research evidence suggests that autistic individuals have higher rates of interaction with the CJS than non-autistic individuals, including a higher likelihood of arrest and caution (Slavny-Cross et al., 2022). However, autistic individuals are no more likely to offend than non-autistic individuals, and are in fact more likely to become victims of crime (National Autistic Society, 2020; Allely, 2022). But, the nature of the criminal justice system in England and Wales creates significant challenges—and possible disadvantages—for autistic individuals suspected, accused or convicted of crimes.

Any individual drawn into criminal proceedings generally faces significant challenges due to their stressful, complex and specialised nature. This is acute for vulnerable persons, including those with physical and mental health issues. However, the neurodevelopmental and behavioural differences in autistic individuals combined with the inherent nature of criminal justice present uniquely challenging obstacles to fairness and effectiveness. Various features of criminal justice processes exemplify this problem. Proceedings often involve verbal interaction; comprise unfamiliar routines and environments, and specialised language; allow the use of non-consensual physical restraint; place emphasis on evaluating behaviour and communication for adjudicative and punitive purposes; and involve chaotic, fast-paced and pressured routines. Autistic individuals may be unable to understand and engage with forms of communication and language used in police stations and court rooms, which will generally be attuned to neurotypical norms, for example, the use of open questions, idiomatic language or abstract concepts. The complexity, length, and stressful nature of proceedings in courts or custody may place strain on the ability of autistic individuals to attend to and engage with what is happening around them (or to them). The physical environments of justice—particularly prisons—may

---

1 Autism can be understood interchangeably with the terms Autism Spectrum Disorder (ASD) and Autism Spectrum Condition (ASC); see section titled 'Language' for a summary of the approach to language in this collection.

place significant sensory demands on autistic individuals; the noise, smell or lighting may result in significant distress and, ultimately, disengagement. All of the above may be very challenging for autistic individuals and therefore present significant barriers to fair, effective and quality engagement.

Until recently, autism in the context of criminal justice had received limited attention outside of academia. The significant but disparate community of (primarily) clinical practitioner researchers providing insight into this area has produced a considerable body of literature over the last two decades,[2] primarily grounded in the disciplines of developmental and forensic psychology. Much of this knowledge base—partly summarised in the previous paragraph—is empirically based, though there still remains significant scope for further research in this area, specifically with direct consideration of the various powers and procedures that comprise the criminal justice system from a socio-legal perspective.[3] Notwithstanding this, there had (until recently) been little policy-level recognition of the issues in this area, with piecemeal and limited integration of knowledge into evidence-led practice, strategy and policy-making. This trend appears to have shifted to some extent; as such, the current policy, practice and research landscape presents—arguably—a golden moment for achieving genuine change in the context of autism and criminal justice.

The last decade has seen important policy developments in relation to the treatment of autistic individuals in a general sense. For example, the passage of the Autism Act in 2009 represented a landmark step in the legislative protection of the rights of autistic individuals. This, in turn, led to the development of the first UK government national strategy for autistic adults, which was later expanded to include children and young people (Department of Education, Department of Health & Social Care, 2021). In terms of criminal justice, increased recognition of the challenges faced by autistic individuals has arguably emerged from wider, critical discourse on the treatment of disability in the criminal justice system. For example, in 2020 the Equality and Human Rights Commission published the findings of an inquiry examining the experiences of disabled defendants and accused persons, concluding that the system was failing this category of vulnerable individuals (EHRC, 2020).

In the same year, the UK government launched a review of neurodiversity in the criminal justice system—including autism as one of the more

2 Some of which is referenced in the Further Recommended Reading.
3 This will be discussed more in the Conclusion.

well-recognised neurodivergent conditions.[4] Reporting in 2021, the review concluded that the system offered 'patchy and inconsistent provision' for neurodivergent individuals, with 'serious gaps, failings, and missed opportunities at every stage of the system' (Criminal Justice Joint Inspection, 2021), thereby suggesting that the criminal justice system remained largely unaffected by many of the insights and recommendations emerging from the research community. Whilst the review recognised signs of progress (particularly in relation to autism), it proposed a series of recommendations designed to introduce a sea change. Nonetheless, the review and the update to the National Autism Strategy in 2021 suggest that much remains to be done to provide autistic individuals with fair and effective access to the criminal justice system (Department of Education, Department of Health & Social Care, 2021).

Scope

With the aforementioned context in mind, this collection provides an up-to-date examination and development of current knowledge in relation to a specific category of vulnerable individuals: autistic suspects, defendants and offenders involved in the criminal justice system of England and Wales. It brings together, in one volume, a diverse and extensive range of existing interdisciplinary research on the domestic criminal justice process and its interaction with autistic accused and convicted people; in short, those who are compulsorily the subject of investigation, trial and punishment. Comprising contributions from a range of expert contributors drawn from academia, clinical practice, forensic psychology and the legal profession, the collection examines knowledge and key themes at different stages of the criminal justice process. Structurally, it broadly follows the typical route through the criminal justice system for individuals accused and convicted of crime, that is, from the earliest stages of contact with police officers; through pre-trial custodial interactions; trials and sentencing; and—in the most severe cases—post-conviction imprisonment. This therefore provides a logical, accessible, focused but comprehensive exploration of the weaknesses and strengths that currently exist across the entire criminal justice system.

Purpose

By explicating the core issues in this important but underexamined area of study in a single place, this collection offers a unique overview of the

---

4 More on this in the concluding section.

challenges for autistic individuals accused or convicted of criminal offences, and incorporates key recommendations for improvement, thereby clarifying the urgent need for substantive changes in policies and practices. It does so at a time of significant change and opportunity in the broad area of autism and criminal justice, providing contemporary and timely insight. Ultimately, it is hoped the collection will help to achieve some of the fundamental aims of most research in this area: to both improve the treatment and experience of autistic people involved in criminal justice processes; and to produce fairer, more appropriate systemic outcomes. Considering the potential far-reaching implications for vulnerable persons (such as autistic individuals) who are investigated, tried and punished, the contributions in this collection provide a vital overview of the core matters of which key stakeholders need to be aware. The collection aims to achieve the following via the chapters presented:

- To explain and explore the unique challenges posed by the nature, structure, and processes of the system for autistic people who are being investigated, prosecuted or punished
- To discuss current problems with the systems and processes in place, and identify good as well as bad practice
- Consider potential and ongoing approaches which could and are adapting and reforming the system to tackle the aforementioned issues, thereby improving the experience of autistic 'subjects' of criminal justice, protecting their individual rights whilst maintaining fair and effective justice outcomes

Language

The matter of language is an important and sensitive one when discussing autism in any academic context. There has been, and continues to be, significant debate about the appropriate language and terminology that should be used when examining this topic, with views often varying depending on the author and their perspective on the topic. For example, there is (generally) a distinction between what might be termed 'person first' (e.g., person with autism) and 'identity first' (e.g., autistic person) construction when writing about autism. Different approaches have arguably legitimate reasons for being used, affecting important matters such as identity, medicalisation, autonomy and stigma. This collection recognises that this remains an open and passionate debate about appropriate language and terminology; and also acknowledges the importance of ensuring academic freedom of expression in writing about autism. As such, this collection does not impose a particular approach to construction; therefore, different chapters may adopt different conventions when describing autism and the quality of being an autistic person. However, contributors have been asked to briefly explain and clarify their approach to language at the start of each chapter; and to remain consistent in their approach throughout their chapter. For more on this issue, please see Vivanti (2020), Botha et al. (2021) and Bottema-Beutel (2021).

Structure and Chapter Summaries

As mentioned earlier, the collection is structured around the major 'stages' of the criminal justice process, exploring the interaction of relevant processes and figures (such as lawyers, police and judges) with autistic suspects, defendants and offenders. Each chapter covers a different stage, starting with autism and 'street' policing in Chapter 1, and proceeding to consider police custody, criminal courts and the post-conviction stage (specifically, prisons). Following is a summary of the content of each chapter.

Chapter 1: '"Street" Policing and Autism: Perceptions and Preconceptions of Police Officers When Interacting with Autistic Suspects in the Community' by Shirley Reveley and Iain Dickie

Chapter 1 offers a critical consideration of how police officers' perceptions of autistic individuals encountered within a community policing context could be affected by the officers' level of awareness and understanding about autism. The first contact for a suspect within the CJS is usually in the community at the time of arrest. As the reported prevalence rate of autism in the community increases, police officers on the beat are increasingly likely to become involved with autistic individuals. Police officers' perceptions and the level of awareness and understanding of autism officers bring to their work has a significant impact on the quality of their interactions with those autistic individuals suspected of committing a crime and impact the outcome. There is a limited amount of research on how differences in perceptual frameworks influence interactions between officers and autistic suspects. Furthermore, frontline officers in England and Wales currently receive limited training on autism, and it is questionable whether this training covers concepts such as perception or empathy. This chapter will propose that autism training for officers on the beat needs to include awareness of perceptual differences and empathetic communication to close what is an identified gap in theory and practice. The chapter reviews police officers' interaction with autistic adults in the 'street' context, followed by a discussion of the adequacy of autism training for police officers. The concept of empathy in the training of police officers will be explored, as well as discussion of how Milton's 'double empathy problem' can help to overcome the empathy divide. The chapter concludes by proposing 'encounter groups' as a useful means of developing mutual understanding of autism between police officers and the autistic community.

Chapter 2: 'Autistic Suspects in Police Custody: Issues Affecting the Effectiveness and Fairness of Police Interviews' by Clare Allely and David Murphy

In the context of police investigation or custodial interview, some autistic individuals may not necessarily be recognised as immediately vulnerable by the police, as a result of their apparent competent use of language and by virtue of the fact that they appear to be intellectually capable. However, despite their apparent abilities, many autistic individuals may experience considerable difficulties in being able to understand and cope with police demands, as well as high levels of distress in the custody context. It is imperative that there is an understanding of the influence that having a diagnosis of autism can have on the investigative interview process given the important function that interviews can have within a number of forensic contexts. For many autistic individuals, a formal interview can cause significant sensory overload and distress, which leads to a negative experience or a poor level of engagement, as well as reducing the quality of information obtained. This chapter will explore how the efficacy of forensic interviews can be affected by features of autism, including detailed discussion of memory impairments; impairment in ability to recall events in a sequential manner; issues with compliance; lack of (or reduced) emotional expression; awkward or inappropriate expressions or behaviours; impaired social communication and interaction; issues with time to respond; misinterpretation or lack of understanding of repetitive interests or behaviours; and unusual ways of speaking. It will conclude by providing a number of recommendations for criminal justice professionals when carrying out investigative interviews with autistic individuals, designed to improve both the experience for suspects and the outcomes.

Chapter 3: 'Autistic Defendants in Court: Perceptions and Support for Accessing Justice' by Clare Allely, Eddie Chaplin, Jody Salter, Jane McCarthy and Felicity Gerry

This chapter serves as both a summary and exploration of the theme that criminal courts—in terms of functions and processes—are not autism-friendly, and that they take insufficient account of autistic defendants' needs. As a result, this not only leads to a negative experience for defendants but also places them at a disadvantage within our adversarial system, undermining their fair-trial rights. This chapter outlines how certain features of ASD may be perceived negatively in the courtroom by criminal justice professionals and decision makers. Case studies are used to explore significant areas of potential vulnerability for autistic defendants, including legislative and procedural disadvantage. The chapter also considers when individuals with ASD are accused of complicity crimes, that is, playing a secondary role in a plan or as an accessory to a crime. Research is lacking as to what extent individuals with ASD may know and understand the essential terms of such a plan or act intentionally in furtherance of someone else's crime, especially when events may be spontaneous where agreement to a plan is alleged to be 'tacit,' or assistance or encouragement is not directed by the principal but said to be the individual intention of the secondary party. The chapter also discusses the role of Liaison and Diversion (L&D) services in the early identification within police stations and their role in supporting defendants with ASD through the court system, recognising the importance of specific expertise being available for clinical assessments to advise the court on appropriate disposal options.

Chapter 4: 'Autism in Prisons: An Overview of Experiences of Custody and Implications for Custodial Rehabilitation for Autistic Prisoners' by Luke P Vinter and Gayle Dillon

Taking a predominantly social model perspective, this chapter aims to introduce and explore some of the challenges faced by autistic individuals serving prison sentences. In addition, the chapter will identify and explore potentially supportive features of prisons for autistic prisoners. The chapter introduces how the social model can develop our understanding of the challenges that autistic individuals may face, before specifically exploring how this could be relevant and understood in a prison context. This is followed by a discussion of some of the most common challenges faced by autistic individuals living in a prison environment. Examples of some of these challenges include difficulties with the social environment, inconsistencies in the prison routine and regime, and aspects of the prison sensory environment. The chapter then considers some elements of prison life that have been found to be supportive features for autistic prisoners. Such features include specialised support provisions, peer support, and additional simple adjustments or accommodations. The chapter also highlights the nuances associated with rehabilitating autistic prisoners in a prison environment, exploring how the prison context can be both supportive and hindering to interventions and rehabilitation for offending behaviours. The chapter concludes with overarching recommendations on how best to work with and support autistic prisoners, with a firm focus on utilising collaborative approaches and listening to the voices of the prison autism community in the design and development of research and practical changes.

The collection closes with a short conclusion chapter, which seeks to both summarise the collection as well as look forward. It first summarises and comments on the major arguments and conclusions presented by the aforementioned chapters, and attempts to identify cross-cutting themes and links that emerge from them. It will proceed to consider the future in relation to autism and criminal justice—specifically in relation to suspects, defendants and offenders—by considering ongoing developments at the time of writing; suggesting some of current gaps in knowledge and understanding which need to be addressed; and highlighting some of the key recommendations for change which should be implemented by policy makers and practitioners.

I hope you enjoy reading this collection of fascinating, research-led insights into a vital and fast-developing area of study, provided by a multidisciplinary group of leaders in their fields. It has been a pleasure and privilege to work with them in bringing it together. I sincerely hope that it will contribute in some way to promoting a much needed evidence-based revolution in the way that autistic individuals are treated by the criminal justice system of England and Wales, and beyond.

1 'Street' Policing and Autism

Perceptions and Preconceptions of Police Officers When Interacting with Autistic Suspects in the Community

Shirley Reveley and Iain Dickie

Introduction

The first contact for a suspect within the criminal justice system (CJS) is usually in the community at the time of arrest (Department of Health, 2009), and as the reported prevalence rate of autism in the community increases (Wallace et al., 2020, p. 1) police officers on the beat are increasingly likely to become involved with autistic individuals (whether as suspects, perpetrators or witnesses to crime). This is a stressful situation for everyone and can be particularly distressing for autistic individuals. Police officers' perceptions and the level of awareness and understanding of autism they bring to their work in the community has a significant impact on the quality of their interactions with those autistic individuals suspected of committing a crime, thus the outcome for those individuals can be positively or negatively affected. Although theories, including Baron-Cohen's theory of mind (1985) and Milton's double empathy hypothesis (2012), have explored differences in perceptual awareness between autistic and neurotypical populations, there remains a limited amount of research on how differences in perceptual frameworks influence the interactions between police officers and individuals with a diagnosis of autism. Furthermore, frontline officers in England and Wales currently receive limited training on autism; the training they do receive is often part of broader sessions on mental health generally, which cover a range of conditions that can be confusing for recipients, meaning training may not be effective (Hepworth, 2017). It is questionable whether this training covers concepts such as perception or empathy, though there is some evidence that this is slowly changing, particularly in the US (Posick et al., 2012; Milton, 2018). This chapter will propose that autism training for officers on the beat—that is, those who work in the community—needs to include awareness of perceptual differences and empathetic communication to close what is an identified gap in theory and practice.

DOI: 10.4324/9781003248774-2

The chapter begins with a review of police officers' interaction with autistic adults in the street situation, drawing on the work of Dickie et al. (2018). There follows a discussion of the UK and US literature on autism training for police officers and the extent to which this is seen to be effective in adequately preparing police officers in interacting with autistic adults. The concept of empathy in the training of police officers will be explored, and then a discussion of how Milton's work on the 'double empathy problem' can help to overcome the empathy divide. Finally, encounter groups are proposed as a useful means of developing a mutual understanding of autism between police officers and the autistic community.

In both the Bradley report (2009) and the report of the Independent Commission on Mental Health and Policing (2013) there is clear acknowledgement of repeated failings in communications between police officers and people with mental ill health and vulnerabilities. Such failings may have led to excessive use of power and resultant trauma for vulnerable individuals. There is now a recognition, as a result of media reports (Lakhini, 2017) and research on this topic, that there is sometimes inappropriate use of force by police with vulnerable individuals, including those who are autistic. As a result, a range of new strategies and guidance have been introduced to train professionals on how to recognise autism and manage professional interactions with autistic people (for example, *The National Strategy for Autistic Children, Young People and Adults: 2021 to 2026*, Department of Health and Social Care & Department for Education, 2021; *Mental Health, Mental Vulnerability and Illness*, College of Policing, 2022). The McGowan training initiative came into law in May 2022 as part of the Health Education England (2022) and is an example of mandatory training for professionals working with people with learning disabilities and autism (NDTI, 2020).

Effective policy frameworks are of course important and necessary for improving interactions between professionals and autistic individuals. However, this chapter will suggest that perception informs the development of policies and practices that underpin the delivery of services to autistic individuals. By *perception* we mean the way in which professionals observe and understand the behaviour and communication of autistic people. Milton (2018) believes that there is a certain amount of complacency surrounding the belief that professionals and practitioners in various contexts (such as healthcare) understand what 'good autism practice' means. He argues that this should never be accepted as a given; rather, development of good autism practice is an 'ongoing, imperfect process of interaction' (Milton, 2018, p. 4) such as that reported by Lakhani (2017). The evidence suggests that police officers on the beat do not have the depth of understanding about autism needed to enable them to appropriately, and fairly, manage their interactions with autistic people in challenging situations such as an arrest or crisis.

'Street' Policing and Autistic Individuals: Current Knowledge

The CJS encompasses initial police contact through the courts and post-conviction or release. A UK autism-specific service provider, All About Autism (Triple A) (2019), has highlighted through feedback from service users and some CJS professionals, that some important gaps in knowledge and understanding of autism exist amongst key CJS providers. This is a key area for investigation and has been studied by academics including Allely and Cooper (2017) and Maras et al. (2016) who discuss how awareness and understanding of autism amongst judicial and legal professionals could affect the services delivered to those identified as being autistic. However, in a systematic literature search of psychological and criminological data-bases, Hepworth (2017) found little research on the initial stages of a criminal investigation; most research focused on other aspects of the process, such as police interview techniques used with autistic suspects, and management of autistic individuals during the trial and imprisonment stages of the system.

For most people, their first interaction with the CJS is usually with officers working in the community, for example, on patrol or for specific call outs. However, little is currently known about how beat officers interact with autistic people and what adaptations, if any, that they make (Crane et al., 2016). In a qualitative study of perceptions of 30 police officers and probation officers in the CJS in the North of England, Dickie et al. (2018) found that some police officers did have general insight into the needs of autistic adults and adjusted their communication with, and approach to, adults they were aware of as being autistic:

> Essentially just trying to adapt your approach to fit them so it might be that you are writing things down, say if it was a victim or witness, allowing them to draw pictures or make diagrams, something like that just so that they didn't have to verbalise perhaps what it was that they were saying.
>
> (Police officer 1)

Hypersensitivity to noise is a feature associated with autism. Bogdashina (2003) recognised that sensitivity to sound, alongside other sensations, has an influence on the cognitive processing style of some autistic individuals. In the study by Dickie et al. (2018), one police respondent showed an understanding of this and the importance of adaptation, specifically by referring to avoiding the use of police sirens when interacting with autistic individuals:

> I wouldn't necessarily put my sirens on when I'm going to somebody. If I'm going to get there one or two minutes earlier, is that really going to be a great deal of help if I'm going to turn up with the sirens on and make things ten times worse, I just don't think that's helpful.
>
> (Police officer 2)

This police officer recognised that an individual with hypersensitivity to noise would react negatively due to the stress caused by the sirens and could lead to panic, running away or aggression, for example.

The preceding examples show that, in theory, it is possible for knowledge and understanding at an abstract level (through training and provision of information) to penetrate everyday police practice. However, the training of officers does not necessarily translate into actual changed behaviour because officers may passively experience training on autism without internalising it and adapting it into changed practice. It is also possible that officers' responses are a result of personal experience of interacting with autistic people rather than the result of training.

It is important to remember that the preceding examples of police officers adapting their behaviours are drawn from a small-scale regional study, and further research is needed into how police officers use both their prior experiences and formalised learning about a social group or culture and apply this to interactions with specific social groups such as autistic individuals. The examples also refer to interactions where it is known that the individual is autistic; however, it is highly likely that during the first encounter between an officer and an individual, the officer may not know the individual is autistic. This raises the issues of identification and disclosure.

Identification and Disclosure of Autism during Police Interactions

Police officers cannot be expected to diagnose autism on first encountering an individual displaying abnormal behaviour such as avoiding eye contact, non-response to questioning, unusual body movements such as flapping, and acts of physical aggression (Hepworth, 2017, p. 2). These behaviours can be interpreted as guilty behaviour and result in inappropriate responses by the police such as excessive force (Independent Commission on Mental Health and Policing, 2013). Hepworth (2017, p. 16) notes that, for autistic individuals, 'there is a reluctance to disclose so the focus must turn to a more understanding culture in which individuals feel they can disclose their diagnosis without fear of negative stereotypes.' Whilst there is little direct evidence on the number of 'street' disclosures of autism to police officers, some research provides insight. In considering the self-declaration of autism in police custody, Crane et al. (2016) found that 37% of the sample of autistic individuals indicated that they did not make their diagnosis known to police at the time of their arrest. The authors suggested the possibility that the autistic individuals did not declare this information to the police as they did not wish to be labelled and treated differently because of their diagnosis of autism. This study clearly highlighted that a significant minority of autistic individuals felt discomfort about making their autism known to officers during street interactions.

The concept of 'context blindness' (Vermeulen, 2012) can be applied to a situation whereby an autistic individual comes into contact with a police officer in the community. That individual might have learnt, perhaps through past experience, that if they are arrested, disclosing their autism diagnosis to a custody officer at the police station may lead to access to guidance and support, for example, through engagement with Liaison and Diversion (L&D) staff (NHS England, 2019).[1] However, that individual might struggle to translate this learning once taken to custody and subsequently being identified as autistic. Thus, the actual number of autistic individuals who choose not to disclose (or aren't identified) is likely to be higher than that identified by Crane et al. (2016) and means that effective training must build opportunities for officers to consider how their own attitudes or beliefs could lead to stereotyping and stigmatisation thereby preventing opportunities for disclosure and identification. A response to the challenge of identification of an individual's autism at the point of contact with police is the Autism Alert Card, which was originally developed through the National Autistic Society as a means for autistic individuals to disclose their autism. Other autistic advocacy services and charities now offer autistic individuals the opportunity to purchase their own Alert Card (NPAA, 2022). The value of an Autism Alert Card is that it can be presented to a police officer thus negating the need for explanation, an important consideration in times of high stress and anxiety in which an autistic person might struggle to verbalise their needs.

1 The aim of the NHS L&D is to identify people with mental health, learning disability, substance misuse or other vulnerabilities coming into contact with the justice system; to assess and refer the identified individual to an appropriate treatment or support service; and to share, with consent, information gained from assessments with criminal justice agencies and the judiciary, so that they can make more informed and timely decisions about out-of-court disposals, case management and sentencing (NHS, 2019).

Vermeulen's (2012) concept of context blindness is relevant here; an autistic person might have learnt that if approached by a police officer at home and by presenting their Autism Alert Card the police officer is made aware of their autism and can make adjustments in response to the situation. However, if approached by a police officer in the street that same individual might not recognise that an opportunity exists to alert the officer to their autism by presenting their card. In short, they may not recognise the benefits of disclosure in this context. Patton (2019) described how autistic people in employment in the US were in a no-win situation, whereby if they do not disclose their autism, they would forgo potentially helpful accommodations that they are entitled to by law; but if they did disclose, they were open to stigmatisation, stereotyping and other negative outcomes. In either scenario, autistic individuals will be subject to attributions and judgments by those who work with them; the same applies for police interactions but arguably with significantly more coercive potential outcomes.

Training on Autism for Police Officers

The ability to identify autism and respond appropriately when it is disclosed returns us to the issue of training and knowledge of officers. In their aforementioned study, Crane et al. (2016) conducted an online survey to elicit the views of 394 police officers from England and Wales, finding that 37% had received training on Autism Spectrum Disorder (ASD) and only 42% were satisfied with how well they had worked with autistic people. Those who had training said that this was mainly aimed at improving their knowledge, communication techniques, and how to minimise stress in the autistic individual. Training was provided by the police service, but 151 officers had not received any training on autism; and most said that general training on ASD, enhanced communication and minimising distress, and specific training for those officers whose role involved working with autistic individuals would be desirable.

The authors also elicited responses from the autistic community and found that they were, in the main, dissatisfied with their experiences of the police and saw the need for more effective training. As a result of their findings, the authors argued that mandatory national evidence-based guidelines and training on autism for police and other CJS professionals were urgently needed. Overall, there is clear evidence of a training gap for officers in terms of both the scope and the type of provision. This is particularly important as officers must be expected to take responsibility for engaging more effectively with autistic individuals in the community due to the communication barriers noted earlier. Whilst there is, generally, a recognition of a need for improvement, little progress was evident beyond greater awareness at the policy-making level of this need, without any substantial action to address issues in practice (Neurodiversity in CJS Review, 2021). As stated earlier, the Oliver McGowan Mandatory Training in Learning Disability and Autism (Health Education England, 2022) is a recent initiative that could well be applied to the training of police officers.

Officer Access to Training on Autism

In their US-based study of law enforcement officers (LEOs) knowledge and awareness of autism, Gardner et al. (2019) state that public awareness campaigns and professional standards have focused on improving knowledge and practice of LEOs in relation to autism. However, it is not clear how well such information is disseminated and how it is incorporated into LEO training. In the context of England and Wales, this was also noted in the aforementioned study by Dickie et al. (2018). In their study, knowledge of autism among respondents was generally described as 'patchy,' with several respondents finding it hard to articulate what autism is. For this group of respondents, training was not provided in a systematic or targeted way, reflecting the findings of Hepworth (2017). Some respondents said that any training on autism was delivered in the context of mental health issues, learning disability or more general issues.

This raises the question of whether officers' understanding was diluted or led to them being overloaded or confused in the sense that police officers may not make the distinction between mental health issues and autism (Hepworth, 2017). It also may have led to negative feelings about training on autism, for example, regarding it as tokenistic being, as it was, just one aspect of training for a larger group of psychological vulnerabilities. The respondents in the study by Dickie et al. (2018) also reported that their training and the dissemination of training opportunities were decided by others, such as senior police personnel:

> Training-wise we don't control the training so that's a sort of barrier, either it's set by headquarters – criminal justice is coming on the next training day. [Name supplied, a training officer] does the area training and he'll pick on certain themes.

This raises the question of how those making such decisions determine which of the various issues covered are important; and whether there is a hierarchy of conditions or whether they are all given equal status. If some conditions are prioritised over others (consciously or not), one must wonder where autism lies in the range of training topics. Arguably, such choices may be driven by current events, politics, policies or police priorities which reassert themselves as important when there is adverse publicity about it (for example, criticisms of stop-and-search practice or issues with disclosure of evidence).

In terms of the nature of the training received, some respondents in the study by Dickie et al. (2018) recognised the need for at least a basic understanding of autism to be provided to officers:

> I haven't had any training on autism or people on the spectrum. I'm talking from a police point of view now. I think police officers need an awareness of people on the autistic spectrum or how they might present. But I do think that being aware is the main thing really, at least having an understanding. I think that's kind of our job really. I think it's a characteristic the police should have anyway.

Other respondents said they would seek out information themselves:

> There's basic training that we all have safeguarding and stuff but I haven't often come across individuals with significant autism that will mean that I would want to go out and or I would need to get that training in order to work with them.

It is interesting to note this respondent's apparent willingness to self-educate but given time pressures and workload issues it is unlikely to be widespread, which perhaps reflects a lower level of importance of training about autism in the overall training portfolio for police officers. This respondent did not expand on what was meant by 'significant autism,' but the term implies an individual who displays overt characteristics of autism or vulnerability.

Other studies, again in the US and in England and Wales, reflect the findings of Dickie et al. (2018) and Hepworth (2017) as regards training. Railey et al. (2020) undertook a qualitative study with 17 participants: six LEOs, six autistic adults, and five caregivers, using semi-structured individual interviews to characterise LEO knowledge of autism; understand interactions between LEOs and autistic individuals; and identify training needs to prepare LEOs for interactions with autistic individuals in the community. All participant groups emphasised the importance of mandatory autism-specific training for LEOs and all suggested recommendations regarding training content and format. What form this content and format would take is not described but implied a need for training that encompasses a diverse array of perspectives and beliefs. It also raises the question of whether the input from autistic individuals and carers, whilst welcome, is sufficient to highlight the diversity of experience across individuals with a diagnosis of autism, which spans all demographic groups and can be highly variable.

Crane et al. (2016) contend that 'lack of appropriate support to individuals with ASD could lead to emotional stress, breakdowns in communication abilities, and behavioural regulation difficulties.' This raises the potential for misinterpretation of behaviours by officers during high-stress or tense situations, as demonstrated by an autistic respondent in Dickie et al. (2019, p. 60):

> OK so contacts where I'm – it's been sort of anxiety, so I can get loud because when talking to the police I might take them literally or not, kind of appear to be contradictory or pedantic or anything like that. ... It might look like kind of like my own kind of knowledge of law and kind of thing, questioning a police officer's behaviour because they weren't necessarily – they were maybe investigating, looking into something, but they weren't so I could easily get into trouble even when I'm – and this has happened with the police, where I've done nothing wrong but my brother, who's a policeman said 'you've just actually talked yourself into a cell.'

This quote highlights the fact that officers need the knowledge and skills to be able to safeguard vulnerable individuals against self-incrimination. This is particularly important because, as Hepworth (2017) points out, autistic individuals can inadvertently put themselves at a disadvantage in certain circumstances such as being cautioned by police. 'A failure to understand this caution, combined with impairments in social communication skills puts those with ASD at risk of self-discrimination, regardless of whether they are incorrectly or correctly accused of a crime' (Hepworth, 2017, p. 5). Young and Brewer (2020) also note that autistic individuals find it difficult to extricate themselves from such situations and allay police suspicions.

Recent official guidance underlines this need for officers to be proactive and aware when engaging with suspects in the community. The College of Policing (2022) in its introduction to *Mental Health, Mental Vulnerability and Illness*, state:

> Early police recognition of the possible mental health problems, learning disabilities or suicidal intent of people they come into contact with is crucial to ensuring an appropriate and effective response.

However, this statement does not explicitly identify neurodevelopmental conditions and as such situates police training for recognition of autism within a too narrow frame of reference. The decision by an officer on first contact with a suspected offender as to whether the person is autistic and/or has some form of mental illness is also important for subsequent decisions in custody. As Parliamentary Under-Secretary for the Home

Office Sarah Newton MP (House of Commons, 2016, Question 56468, reported in House of Commons, 2018) said in answer to a question on places of safety:

> If a person with ASD appears to be suffering from a mental disorder and is deemed in need of immediate care and control, a police officer may remove that person to a place of safety under section 135 and 136 of the Mental Health Act 1983. If a person with ASD does not appear to be suffering from a mental disorder and is not in need of care and control, a place of safety as defined under the Mental Health Act (1983) would not be an appropriate environment. In these cases, appropriate alternative measures of support should be sought in line with the needs of that individual.

This raises two important questions. First, how does a police officer in the street decide if a person is mentally ill or displaying autistic behaviours when the person is acting bizarrely? Second, what are 'appropriate alternative measures of support'? It would seem that, in the first instance, advice should be sought from an appropriate professional. The College of Policing (2022, p. 2) states that decision-making by the police on the most appropriate course of action should be guided by the National Decision Model (NDM):

> Decision making concerning health care matters should be made by clinically trained professionals and not police officers. When police officers are called to respond to a situation involving a mentally vulnerable person, it is important that they have access relevant information that may inform risk management. They should seek guidance from health care professionals where appropriate. Police actions and interventions should be proportionate to the requirement, using the least restrictive means to protect the safety of the individual, the public and themselves, and to prevent crime.

However, it needs to be acknowledged that it is probably unrealistic for police officers involved in a crisis situation to gain expert advice in a timely manner, not least because of the need to manage immediate issues. The following paragraph usefully highlights the challenges awaiting officers responding to incidents within the community and the need to consider whether an individual is autistic or whether there might be other factors to consider:

> Officers should also consider the possible explanations for an individual's behaviour, including physical illness, injury or neuro-disability, mental

ill health, a learning disability and intoxication (caused by medication, illicit drugs or alcohol). Mental health problems and illness exist along a continuum of severity and even those with severe and enduring mental illness may have episodes of functioning very well and may have episodes of crisis.

(College of Policing, 2022)

It is also worth noting that this section does acknowledge 'neuro-disability,' an umbrella term for a range of neurodevelopmental differences, suggesting a more nuanced context for such guidance.

Notwithstanding this, the guidance does highlight the somewhat arbitrary approach to distinguishing individuals who are 'mentally vulnerable' (and thus in need of protection) and individuals who are 'suspicious or criminal' (who are not). It ignores the possibility that an individual may be suspicious but vulnerable (and therefore still in need of protection); and if they are vulnerable but not suspicious, that this vulnerability will be reasonably obvious.

The national autism strategy (Department of Health and Social Care & Department for Education, 2021) and Criminal Justice Joint Inspection (CJJI, 2021) acknowledge autism in its own right rather than in terms of mental illness or learning disability, and both recognise the need for national standards of training across the criminal justice system. The CJJI (2021) recommended

a programme of awareness-raising and specialist training should be developed and delivered to staff working within criminal justice services. For frontline staff this learning should be broad-based, mandatory, raise awareness of neurodivergent conditions and how they impact on communication and be supported by practical strategies for working with neurodivergent people. More specialised training should be provided for staff whose roles require it. The programme should be developed and delivered in consultation with people who have personal experience of neurodivergence.

The national autism strategy states:

By 2026, we want to have made improvements in autistic people's experiences of coming into contact with the criminal and youth justice systems, by ensuring that all staff understand autism and how to support autistic people.

(Section 8)

More broadly, the strategy also proposes 'the development of a toolkit to educate frontline staff about neurodiversity, and the additional support people might need.' With specific reference to police officers, the strategy acknowledges the fact that autistic people are not always treated fairly and that there is a need to divert suspects with autism away from the CJS if it is appropriate to do so:

> We also want to ensure police officers understand autistic people's specific needs – for example around communication and sensory needs – and the reasonable adjustments they might need to make to standard police practices, as this is crucial in ensuring autistic people are treated fairly and are appropriately diverted away from the criminal and youth justice systems where possible and appropriate.
>
> (Section 8)

The aspirations of this strategy are laudable; but there is no detail on how the strategy will be delivered, leaving this important aspect to the relevant organisations to implement. It is probable that education and training will follow established and known patterns, such as developing workbooks, when what is required are innovative approaches that include face-to-face interactions with autistic people. Therefore, though training is available to police officers (as detailed earlier), the consistency, depth and focus of such training remain unclear.

Furthermore, opportunities for learning and reflection are mainly one-sided, meaning that opportunities for learning about autism are located within individual police forces and may be limited in scope. Opening a dialogue between officers and autistic self-advocates would allow for a better understanding of officers about any fears or concerns autistic people might have regarding contact with police or allay misunderstandings about the nature of the community-facing officers' work. Bridging perceptual barriers between autistic and neurotypical individuals requires opportunities to engage with one another to better understand and empathise with the others' perspectives. Examples of engagement include public engagement groups (HMCTS, 2022) and Officer Friendly Day in Michigan (Singh, 2022). This sort of collaborative approach is very important to building the confidence of an affected community in the legitimacy of training and knowledge, but also in helping officers make their understanding concrete rather than abstract.

Training Police Offers for Empathy

Training for understanding perceptions and empathy is not mentioned specifically in any of the aforementioned research papers or strategies, nor is there any detail in the national autism strategy (Department of Health and Social

Care & Department for Education, 2021) as to what form the training will take and the indication of content is presented in very broad terms. It will be interesting to see whether new training programmes will include aspects of empathy and perception training, as is now happening in parts of the US (Posick et al., 2012; Suttie, 2016). Empathy refers to a person's ability to understand the emotions of others and share in their feelings (Posick et al., 2012). It is increasingly being recognised that empathy matters in crime and punishment, and research in the US suggests juvenile delinquency can be reduced by taking certain steps, for example, relationships between communities and police can be improved by empathy training. Posick et al. (2012) reviewed what is currently known about empathy and perceptions of empathy in crime and justice. They found that when factors like age, sex, race, education and income are taken into account, empathetic people are less likely to engage in delinquency or crime; empathy affects how people think about crime and punishment in complex ways; empathy and perceptions of empathy help to shape the interactions of police and members of the communities they are assigned to protect. They also posited that empathy training in training curricula can furnish officers with ways to be more effective and improve community reactions to their efforts. Such training will include steps to help officers learn about empathy and show empathy for the concerns of the specific communities where they work. Showing empathy is said to increase trust and confidence in the police and greater trust results in getting more cooperation in daily interactions with citizens. As a result, officers then find it easier to protect themselves and the communities in which they work (Posick et al., 2012).

Empathy also has a relationship with confidence in policing. Suttie (2016) discusses this in the context of police killings of unarmed black citizens in the US, arguing that such incidents lead to fundamental questions about the integrity of the police. The aftermath of the George Floyd murder and the subsequent intense scrutiny of policing in the US and beyond is a good example of this. Equally, retribution killings of innocent police officers resulting from such incidents create fear for their own safety at work. Suttie cites a 2012 Gallup Poll that shows that confidence in the police had dropped to its lowest level in 22 years. However, Suttie contends that research gives cause for hope, as some of the findings suggest that helping police officers to slow down in their encounters with the public and to practice more respectful and empathic communication could help reduce excessive force and unnecessary arrests. These arguments suggest that training officers for empathy could be a worthwhile step in the right direction for officers engaging with autistic individuals. However, such training has serious limitations, as it is based on neurotypical perceptions and may therefore render such training ineffective without accounting for what Milton (2012) describes as the double empathy problem.

The Double Empathy Problem and the Implications for Police Officer Training

According to Heyworth (2020), non-autistic people perceive autistic people as lacking empathy, which, as was defined above, centres on the ability to see interactions from another's perspective and understand the emotions involved (Suttie, 2016). Additionally, a long-standing theory related to autism and perception is the concept of impaired theory of mind (ToM; Baron-Cohen et al., 1985). ToM posits that people can have different thoughts, feelings and perspectives relating to a situation, but understanding and recognising this can be challenging for an autistic person as they lack the ability to imagine the thoughts and feelings of others. As a result, this makes it difficult for autistic individuals to predict the actions and intentions of others. However, Milton (2012) has argued that the traditional understanding and application of ToM is inaccurate, arguing:

> The 'theory of mind' and 'empathy' so lauded in normative psychological models of human interaction, refers to the ability a 'neuro-typical' (NT) individual has to assume understandings of the mental states and motives of other people. When such 'empathy' is applied toward an 'autistic person' however, it is often wildly inaccurate in its measure. Such attempts are often felt as invasive, imposing and threatening by an 'autistic person,' especially when protestations to the contrary are ignored by the NT doing the 'empathising.'

Instead, Milton asserts that it is equally challenging for neurotypical people to accurately interpret a situation from the perspective of an autistic individual, as empathy is, in reciprocal interactions, a two-way process. For Milton (2018), the double empathy problem relates to 'a breach in the natural attitude that occurs between people of different dispositions outlooks and personal conceptual understandings when attempts are made to communicate meaning.' In short, it is a 'double' problem because both individuals experience it, not just one person. As a result, 'when people with different experiences of the world interact, they will struggle to empathise with each other,' an issue which is further complicated by other differences such as language or comprehension (Milton, 2018).

In explaining Milton's double empathy problem, Heyworth (2020) argues that autistic experiences lead to different life experiences which create an 'empathy divide.' If autistic people lack insight into neurotypical culture, it is equally arguable that neurotypical people lack insight into the culture and communication of autistic people. The empathy divide is then experienced by both parties, but these groups are affected unequally by the divide. Milton (2012) says that non-autistic people assume that their way of empathising is superior to, or preferable to, that of autistic people; this suggests that non-autistic people lack empathy for autistic people and expect autistic people to adapt to and conform with non-autistic culture and communication styles. Conversely, non-autistic people do not expect to have to learn and understand autistic perceptions. In this sense, ToM (as traditionally understood) takes a fundamentally neurotypical perspective and is therefore a biased method of understanding autism and interactions with autistic individuals.

Milton's double empathy theory represents an important challenge to the traditionally accepted lack of ToM in autistic people and 'reframes the disjunct between autistic and non-autistic communities. Instead of seeing superior and inferior ways of being we can see our co-existence as reliant on reciprocity and mutuality' (Heyworth, 2020).

Perceptions, Stigma and Attribution

Training of officers should also consider the role of perception management, stigma and attribution in interactions between autistic individuals and others. In a US study exploring LEO awareness and knowledge of autism, Gardner et al. (2019) found that the officers reported feeling better equipped to respond to calls involving autistic individuals when they had attended training programmes that gave them knowledge and awareness of autism. LEOs need to recognise symptoms and characteristics of autism and be able to respond appropriately to those individuals demonstrating symptoms, therefore, knowledge of and training related to autism is essential (Gardner et al., 2019). However, the authors point out that perceptions of officers regarding autistic individuals are still an underresearched area, and that further research into appropriate training content—as well as the perceptions of autistic individuals regarding their interactions with officers—is needed.

Perceptions lead to stereotyping and stigmatisation, which Goffman (1963) described as being where a person's social identity does not fit that expected in a particular context. Patton (2019) contends that ASD is a neurological disorder, those who suffer from it being subject to stereotypes and fears that result in stigmatising both autism as a condition and the people who live with it. Citing studies of stigma, Patton argues that neurological and psychological disorders such as autism are stigmatised primarily due to fear, with individuals in this category being seen as incompetent, awkward, cold, unsociable, and possibly as aggressive or dangerous. These perceptions lead to negative outcomes for individuals from disadvantaged groups. As a consequence, Patton points out that there are strategies disadvantaged people use to actively manage others' perceptions and therefore mitigate negative outcomes, for example, picking up on non-verbal cues or correcting what the police officer might be mistakenly assuming about a situation. The problem is that strategies available to groups with less power, such as racial minorities and the elderly, are not likely to be accessible to autistic individuals due to challenges with social communication, acting as a barrier to management of the negative perceptions and experiences.

Attribution theory and research has shown that if a person's behaviours are consistent over time, observers will be more confident and certain in their attributions of that person (Patton, 2019). However, autistic behaviours and characteristics that are often unusual and inconsistent are likely to engender different (often negative) attributional processes on the part of co-workers, managers and other observers (Patton, 2019). Patton (2019) was concerned with autistic individuals' experiences in the workplace, but his work can equally be related to perceptions and attributions in a wider context, including interactions with police officers. He argues that many autistic workers display behaviours that stand in opposition to those traditionally believed to be those of a 'good employee,' for example, someone who can communicate effectively, interact with others as part of a team and possess emotional intelligence. These characteristics might also be regarded as those of a 'good citizen.' If an autistic individual is unable to outwardly demonstrate or display these characteristics in a stressful situation such as an interaction or confrontation with an officer on the beat, this can lead to a negative perception of that individual as frustrating, aggressive or non-compliant. This is likely to be exacerbated in particular stressful encounters (e.g., when there is perception of violence, or some other form of crisis situation). This can, in turn, lead to negative attributions by police officers and may have a deleterious effect on the outcome of the encounter.

Bridging an Empathic Divide

The double empathy hypothesis asserts that acknowledging differences in perceptual frameworks is a two-way process: it is as much the responsibility of neurotypical individuals to understand the lived experience of autistic individuals, as it is for autistic individuals to consider neurotypical perceptions. Taking this into account, we suggest that the creation of workbooks, whilst important and useful, does not offer sufficient opportunities for serving officers to understand the thoughts, feelings and perspectives of autistic individuals, and the reasons why an individual might withhold or disclose their diagnosis to a police officer. Opportunities to consider the lived perspectives of autistic and neurotypical people could be made more available and accessible through 'encounter groups.' The idea of encounter groups is derived from the work of psychotherapist and academic Carl Rogers (1970), who originally conceived such groups as an unstructured opportunity for individuals to meet and hear the thoughts, feelings and perspectives of others within the group. In Rogerian or person-centred terms, the opportunity for an 'encounter' is to learn about ourselves and how our thoughts, feelings and perspectives could parallel or differ from others.

Roger's facilitation of group encounters led to some powerful encounters between individuals and groups who often held polarising and contradictory positions. For example, meetings between a range of communities in apartheid South Africa and in Northern Ireland in the 1970s and early 1980 engaged with particularly controversial and emotive topics. Roger's examples of encounters are more historic, but Haley and Yates (2020) have explored the power of group encounters in a modern context in London-based counselling students, highlighting the effect on the group of being enabled to meet with others from, at times, radically different cultural frameworks. Whilst these examples deal with different contexts, they raise the question of the potential for autistic and neurotypical individuals to meet to consider the lived experiences and perceptual differences of each other. In the context of autistic individuals and police officers, this could enable a richer understanding of how interactions could have hidden challenges and complexities not otherwise realised.

Rogers felt that meeting others without a preconceived agenda offered valuable opportunities for personal as well as social growth and development. However, in recognition of some of the challenges relating to executive functioning that can be experienced by neurodiverse populations, the idea of a Rogerian unstructured encounter between police officers and autistic individuals could be undermined by barriers to communication and learning. In seeking to create a learning environment that facilitates meaningful opportunities for exchange of views and perspectives among encounters between police officers and autistic individuals, any encounter group would need some structure or agenda to avoid or minimise any undue distress caused by the uncertainty created by an unstructured encounter. Therefore, we would suggest that encounters between community-facing police officers, autistic individuals and family members, with opportunities for individuals to submit questions or themes for discussion, could assist in demystifying police interactions.

For example, it could allow autistic individuals to better understand the reasons why an officer working in the community might ask specific questions or take certain actions. It could also allow an opportunity for police officers to understand the legitimate fears or apprehensions that might prevent an autistic person from disclosing their diagnosis. The idea of pre-planned encounters between police officers and members of the community is undoubtedly challenging in terms of resourcing; however, if appropriately planned and facilitated, such forms of learning could emphasise the humanity of all concerned and enhance empathy and understanding in ways that a textbook or online continuing professional development (CPD) never could achieve. An example of police officers engaging with autistic people and their families in Michigan, USA, is Officer Friendly Day during Autism Acceptance Month where the families and officers interacted in a day of fun (April 6, 2022).

Conclusion

The authors support research findings that current training curricula for police officers are insufficient in adequately preparing them for effective interactions with autistic adults: it is not enough to provide them with a checklist of dos and don'ts. Drawing on Milton's double empathy hypothesis we posit that greater emphasis should be placed on increasing officers' awareness of perceptual differences to facilitate greater empathy and understanding of autistic and neurotypical perceptual frameworks. Raising awareness of the fact that empathy is a two-way process is crucial and, though important and helpful, checklists are but a part of the toolkit required for effective interactions.

Milton (2012) contends that the difference in perceptual frameworks between autistic and neurotypical people is that both groups can at times struggle to accurately perceive and appreciate the perspectives of the other group. In considering problems of communication, it is important not to apportion blame through a discussion of deficits but to appreciate how differences in communication style and perception can create unintended barriers to effective communication and lead to increased levels of stress and anxiety for service users and CJS professionals alike. This is important not only because it can lead to unfair experience, but potentially to inaccurate or ineffective CJS outcomes such as unnecessary arrest or use of force.

Whilst the authors acknowledge that professionals working within the CJS (e.g., police or probation services) are legally obliged to abide by a set of rules in their interactions with service users such as the revised PACE C Code of Conduct that relate to the arrest, questioning and detention of suspects in custody, the evidence discussed in this chapter shows that some professionals can, and are, adapting their communication style to accommodate the different perceptual frameworks of autistic individuals. It remains challenging to definitively assess how widely and effectively opportunities for learning are being offered across police forces throughout England and Wales. It also remains problematic for training designed to build understanding and acceptance to be purely located within an organisation or community, without the involvement and input of those with lived experience.

Using the idea of encounter groups, we suggest that there are significant benefits to providing pre-planned opportunities for autistic and neurotypical individuals across both police forces and local communities to meet and engage. Such encounters would allow both autistic individuals and officers to share thoughts, feelings and perspectives related to autism, neurodiversity and the ways in which police officers might respond in particular situations. Facilitating such opportunities would help to bridge the empathic divide created by the double empathy problem, thus improving training for officers in the context of autism and instilling more confidence in the autistic community that officers will be able to appropriately engage with them.

2 Autistic Suspects in Police Custody

Issues Affecting the Effectiveness and Fairness of Police Interviews

Clare Allely and David Murphy

Introduction

In the context of police investigation or custodial interview, some autistic individuals[1] may not necessarily be recognised as immediately vulnerable by the police, as a result of their apparent competent use of language and by virtue of the fact that they appear to be intellectually capable. However, despite their apparent abilities, many autistic individuals may experience considerable difficulties in being able to understand and cope with police demands. They may also face high levels of distress in the context of the closed social situation of an investigative interview (North et al., 2008). It is imperative that there is an understanding of the influence that having a diagnosis of autism can have on the investigative interview process given the important function that interviews can have within a number of forensic contexts (see, for example, Nesca & Dalby, 2013; Murphy, 2018). For many autistic individuals, a formal interview can cause significant sensory overload and distress which leads to a negative experience or a poor level of engagement, as well as reducing the quality of information obtained. In some forensic contexts, it is possible that these reactions to sensory overload are misinterpreted by interviewers as indications of guilt or deliberate acts of anti-social behaviour (see Debbaudt, 2002; Murphy, 2018).

A number of other features associated with autism—such as memory impairments and impairment in ability to recall events in a sequential manner, among numerous others which will be discussed in this chapter—can also be misinterpreted in a negative way (or considered evidence of evasion or guilt) by criminal justice professionals in an investigating interview

---

1 Terminology for describing individuals with autism varies, however, evidence suggests that 'autistic' is the preferred term by a large number of individuals and their families (Kenny et al., 2015).

DOI: 10.4324/9781003248774-3

context, perhaps resulting in being more likely to provide false admissions, being charged and subsequently convicted, etc. This chapter will explore how the efficacy of forensic interviews can be affected by features of autism, including detailed discussion of memory impairments, impairment in ability to recall events in a sequential manner, issues with compliance, lack of (or reduced) emotional expression, awkward or inappropriate expressions or behaviours, impaired social communication and interaction, issues with time to respond, misinterpretation or lack of understanding of repetitive interests or behaviours, and unusual ways of speaking. The chapter will conclude by providing a number of recommendations for criminal justice professionals when carrying out an investigative interview with autistic individuals.

Autism is a neurodevelopmental disorder characterised by recipro-cal social interaction and communication impairments and also restricted repetitive behaviours. Described as Autism Spectrum Disorders, the fifth edition of the *Diagnostic and Statistical Manual of Mental Disorders* characterises two core areas of impairment in autism, namely, (1) 'per-sistent deficits in social communication and social interaction' and (2) 'restricted, repetitive patterns of behaviour, interests, or activities' (APA, 2013). Repetitive behaviours and restricted interests (RBRIs) charac-terise behaviours that can include repetitive motor movements, sensory reactions, rituals, routines and restricted interests. It is common to think of an individual's autism as being on a spectrum (ranging from severely impaired to mildly impaired). However, it is more appropriate and accu-rate to consider that autistic individuals have a profile which includes both strengths and weaknesses. A highly functioning autistic individual has a profile of both strengths and weaknesses. The particular strengths in many high-functioning autistic individuals can make them appear to others to be relatively unimpaired. However, certain strengths in what is stereotypi-cally perceived to be a high-functioning individual can mask significant impairments or weaknesses, which can be potentially detrimental to that individual in given certain situations. As such, there is a need to move away from the misconception that 'mild' or 'high-functioning' autism does not have severe consequences, particularly in a forensic context (Allely, 2022). Professionals carrying out investigative interviews with autistic individuals need to recognise and be aware that just because the individual gives the appearance of social engagement and understanding, this does not auto-matically mean that they actually understand the specific circumstances of the situation or context they are in (Dickie et al., 2018).

Prevalence of Autism in the Context of Police Interactions

It is important to emphasise in any discussion around autism and the crimi-nal justice system that autistic individuals are no more likely to engage in offending behaviour when compared to the general population (King & Murphy, 2014; Rutten et al., 2017). Indeed, whilst some evidence suggests that autistic individuals are more likely to be a victim of an offence (Weiss & Fardella, 2018), there is a small subgroup who do offend. It is important that there is consideration around how certain features of autism may be a contributing factor or provide the context of vulnerability to both engaging in the offending behaviour and subsequent involvement in criminal justice processes. The core domains of impairment or features of autism (impairments in social communication and social interaction, preference for sameness, fixated interests, and hyper- and hyporeactivity to sensory stimulus) (APA, 2013) may contribute to the high rates of involvement with police across a number of specific contexts. Several studies have examined the number of autistic individuals who come into contact with the criminal justice system. For instance, in one Canadian study, a survey of 35 autistic adults aged between 18 and 65 years showed that 80% reported at least one interaction with police in their lifetime (Salerno & Schuller, 2019). The findings also revealed that 39% of the adults in the survey reported four to nine interactions with police and 14% reported experiencing ten or more interactions with police (Salerno & Schuller, 2019).

A study carried out in the US using a nationally representative sample of youth with autism found that by the age of 21 about 20% had interacted with law enforcement officers (Rava et al., 2017). Specifically, the study investigated whether youth, at both 14–15 years old and 21–22 years old, had been stopped and questioned by police or arrested. A total of 11,270 youth nationwide were enrolled into the study, of which 920 had a diagnosis of autism. By age 21, 19.5% of youth with autism had been stopped and questioned by police. Almost a quarter of those individuals who were stopped and questioned by police had never been arrested (4.7%). It was also found that nearly half of all the individuals who had ever been stopped and questioned by police had experienced this by the time they were 15 years old. Youth were found to be more likely involved in the criminal justice system if they displayed externalising behaviours (Rava et al., 2017). These findings of arrest rates in autistic individuals are consistent with a number of other studies (Brookman-Frazee et al., 2009; Cheely et al., 2012; Tint et al., 2017). In summary, a range of studies suggest that many autistic individuals, especially young adults, have an increased vulnerability with having contact with the police.

Common Features of Autism That Need to be Considered During Investigative Interviews

On the basis that, in specific contexts, engagement with the police as a suspect is more likely for autistic individuals, it is important to consider what, if any, role their diagnosis may play in subsequent interactions. In a recent study, Gibbs and Haas (2020) sought to explore and describe the impact that autistic characteristics (that is, core features of autism, as described earlier; and co-occurring conditions such as attention deficit hyperactivity disorder [ADHD]) may have in such interactions, via interviews with 12 autistic adults and 19 parent/carers about interactions with police in the past five years. In the vast majority (92.3%) of the 39 police interactions which were described by participants, one or more of the individuals' autistic characteristics (notably the interpersonal communication difficulties) were described as having a role in their interaction with police (Gibbs and Haas, 2020). There are some common features of autism that need to be considered by police during investigative interviews. The ones we will focus on in this chapter include memory impairments, impairment in ability to recall events in a sequential manner, issues with compliance, lack of (or reduced) emotional expression, awkward or inappropriate expressions or behaviours, impaired social communication and interaction, issues with time to respond, misinterpretation or lack of understanding of repetitive interests or behaviours, and unusual ways of speaking.

Memory Impairments

Some autistic individuals may be more vulnerable during investigative interviewing because of memory impairments (for example, Bowler et al., 1997; Bigham et al., 2010; Boucher et al., 2012; Maister et al., 2013). Research has found that many autistic individuals have difficulties in recollecting or remembering past personally experienced events, tend to remember fewer of them and also take more time to do this compared to individuals without autism (Goddard et al., 2007; Crane et al., 2012). Additionally, studies have revealed that, when compared to individuals without autism, autistic individuals have a tendency to rely on feelings of familiarity to guide their memory (Bowler et al., 2000; see also Maras & Bowler, 2012; Johnson et al., 2018). With regard to their memory for semantic and general information (that is, knowledge-based information), autistic individuals are usually unimpaired. However, autistic individuals often need much more prompting in order to retrieve specific episodes, that is, memory for specific events, known as episodic memory (Crane & Goddard, 2008; Bigham et al., 2010; Crane & Maras, 2018). Within an investigative interview, it is possible that these forms of memory characteristics may be perceived as being invasive and that an individual is reluctant to reveal personal information.

Impairment in Ability to Recall Events in a Sequential Manner

Autistic individuals can often be perceived, erroneously, as being uncooperative and non-responsive during investigative interviews with police as they can frequently experience impairments in their ability to recall events in a sequential manner and with sufficient detail. When asked to report the sequence of events of the day or time being investigated, for example, they may exhibit difficulties in recalling and reporting the exact sequence of events in the order that they took place (Kroncke et al., 2016). Perception of time has also been found to be altered in autistic individuals (see, for example, Jurek et al., 2019). It is also useful for police investigative interviews to recognise that some autistic individuals can also have an impaired ability to determine how long specific events lasted. For instance, an autistic individual may have difficulty responding to questions such as, 'How long did you walk in the park before you went to your friend's house?' These particular impairments may make an autistic individual appear evasive; an officer might incorrectly believe the autistic individual is attempting to hide something rather than it being a genuine difficulty in being able to recall this information (Goddard et al., 2007; Crane et al., 2012). In other words, the officer may conclude that the individual is getting the timing and order of events wrong because they are lying about the events. As a result, an individual is more likely to be considered to be guilty of the suspected offence being investigated, with negative outcomes such as a charge.

Issues with Compliance

It is increasingly recognised that, although autistic individuals are not more suggestible when compared to those without autism, they are found to exhibit greater levels of compliance, eagerness to please and avoidance of confrontation (North et al., 2008; Chandler et al., 2019). Given that autistic individuals, when compared to individuals without autism, are often more compliant, fearful and deferential when they are asked questions by persons in authority (Freckelton, 2013) such as police officers, they may be at increased risk of complying with the pressures of an investigative interview. This common feature in autistic individuals can lead them to make statements which are erroneous and self-incriminating during investigative interviews (Gudjonsson, 2003), or respond compliantly to the interviewer's requests and demands, despite not agreeing with the information or believing it to be inaccurate (Maras & Bowler, 2012). Again, this may lead to inaccurate admissions or the acceptance of unreasonable conditions or expectations (for example, longer detention or waiver of legal representation). Therefore, heightened compliance places autistic individuals at risk of unfair outcomes or even miscarriages of justice.

In their study, North and colleagues (2008) compared 26 individuals with high-functioning autism,[2] with 27 gender- and IQ-matched control groups on measures of interrogative suggestibility using the Gudjonsson Suggestibility Scale 2 (GSS 2) (Gudjonsson, 1997) and on compliance using the Gudjonsson Compliance Scale (GCS) (Gudjonsson, 1989). The Paranoia Scale (Fenigstein & Vanable, 1992) was used to measure anxiety levels, depression levels, the extent to which the participants feared negative evaluation by others and trait suspiciousness/tendencies to mistrust others. The high compliance score found in the autism group members, compared to the gender- and IQ-matched controls, would indicate that they are more easily led, manipulated or coerced by others into engaging in behaviours which are illegal (Gudjonsson et al., 2004). Autistic individuals may be more predisposed towards compliance with a desire to please the interviewer due to impaired social skills (Maras & Bowler, 2012), a feature of autism which can result in elevated levels of social anxiety (Kuusikko et al., 2008). Higher levels of compliance may cause an autistic individual, during an investigative interview, to feel pressured into agreeing to incriminating statements that are incorrect or to confess to something they have not done simply to escape the situation as soon as possible (Gudjonsson, 2003).

Lack of (or Reduced) Emotional Expression

Autistic individuals often have impaired theory of mind (ToM) abilities, which can have a potential impact on engagement with police officers during investigative interviews. ToM refers to the ability to ascribe mental states (such as beliefs, desires, intentions and emotions) to both oneself and others in order to understand and predict behaviour (Baron-Cohen et al., 1985). Given the potential for impaired ability to appreciate the subjective experiences of others, autistic individuals may not exhibit any outward expressions of empathy or intersubjective resonance (even if they are feeling it internally). This can lead to misinterpretation, by others, of what an autistic individual is thinking or feeling. In the context of an investigative interview, this can lead police officers to incorrectly assume that the interviewee is cold, calculating and remorseless (Allely & Cooper, 2017), with the inevitable inference that they are guilty of the suspected offence. Young and Brewer (2019) investigated whether perspective-taking

---

2 The term used in the study, but note the caution expressed in the introduction to this chapter regarding the terms 'high' and 'low' functioning.

impairments could predict difficulty for autistic individuals extricating themselves from situations where police officers suspected them of a crime they did not commit. Their sample comprised 32 individuals (12 females and 20 males) with a diagnosis of autism or Asperger syndrome (AS), covering a range of ages, from 20 to 64 years old (with a mean age of 33.3 years and standard deviation of 13.8 years). Findings from the sample group were compared to a typically developing control group, which included 41 English-speaking individuals (26 females and 15 males) who were enrolled in undergraduate or tertiary transition programmes. In the typically developing control group, the age range was 17 to 49 years (with a mean age of 21.7 years and standard deviation of 5.9 years).

Both groups in the study were asked to listen to scenarios in which they were placed in situations where the police believed, erroneously, that they had been involved in crime. In every scenario given to all participants, there was critical information included that, if the participants recognised it and provided this information to the police, it would confirm that they had nothing to do with the crime. In short, the scenarios tested the ability of participants to identify what the police would consider important information pertaining to innocence, therefore requiring a degree of perspective-taking. Compared to the controls, the adults with autism were found to perform markedly worse on perspective-taking measures and the extrication task (Young & Brewer, 2019), with difficulty in identifying the aforementioned information and—as a result—being less able to allay suspicions of criminality. In an applied setting such as a police interview, such failures to judge relevant information required to extricate themselves from a situation may result in an individual being perceived as guilty.

Awkward or Inappropriate Expressions or Behaviours

Perhaps linked to difficulties with making accurate inferences about the mental states of others, in some situations autistic individuals may display awkward or inappropriate facial expressions or behaviours during a police interview (for example, laughing or smiling whilst being asked questions about their alleged offending behaviour). This can happen more frequently during stressful situations, which a police investigative interview would typically be for most people. However, this outward expression may not represent what they are feeling internally (Allely & Cooper, 2017). Unusual or inappropriate expressions and behaviours serve as a coping strategy when people with autism find themselves in situations they do not understand, or when they do not know what is expected of them. For example, in *Sultan v R* ([2008] EWCA Crim 6), an autistic defendant read a book whilst his alleged victim was undergoing questioning on the stand. The jury was unaware of his diagnosis, and he was convicted. The defendant challenged this, with the Court of Appeal concluding that if the jury had heard evidence of the defendant's autism (specifically, Asperger syndrome) it 'might have gone some way to explain to the jury why the appellant was behaving so oddly at trial, such as reading a book during [the complainant's] evidence' (Cooper & Allely, 2017). This could, therefore, have had a material impact on the jury's assessment of the defendant's guilt. The potential for similar misinterpretation and consequences is clear in the context of investigative interviews.

Impaired Social Communication and Interaction

Impairments in social communication and interaction are found in all autistic individuals. They may interrupt the police officer during the investigative interview with no understanding or appreciation of the likely negative reactions to such behaviour. Such behaviour would be viewed by police as evasive, rude, arrogant or considered as evidence of a lack of willingness to cooperate. Impairments in the use of gestures, understanding personal space, timing, topic selection and difficulties with understanding non-literal language (such as metaphors, irony, sarcasm or humour) may also be found in many autistic individuals (Allely & Cooper, 2017). Many autistic individuals understand language in a very literal and concrete way and may take things at face value, rather than understanding the way the meaning of the words is affected by other factors (including facial expression, tone of voice, non-verbal cues/body language and the context). All of these factors may combine to present significant barriers to autistic individuals understanding the nature of questioning and how to respond. Moreover, some autistic individuals can also be hesitant to seek clarification on something they do not understand. As a result, officers are unlikely to recognise and adapt to such challenges.

Issues with Time to Respond

When asked a question, many autistic individuals need additional time to allow them to process verbal information and to give an answer (Crane & Maras, 2018; Murphy, 2018) irrespective of whether they are traditionally considered high-functioning or not, as processing time is not related to intelligence. This need for more time to process verbal information is often referred to as 'Asperger time' (Jacobsen, 2003; Myles et al., 2005). It is important that autistic individuals are given, if required, more time to consider and respond to questions during an investigative interview (Kroncke et al., 2016). Failure to consider or provide an individual with sufficient time to process and respond to questions during an interview may result in anxiety for the individual, as well as poor quality and unreliable information.

Misinterpretation or Lack of Understanding of Repetitive Behaviours and Restricted Interests

As mentioned at the start of the chapter, RBRIs are a common feature of autism. If the repetitive interest or particular obsession is displayed by an autistic individual—either during the investigative interview or as part of alleged offending behaviour—this may be misinterpreted or misunderstood. Some of the kinds of repetitive behaviours that may be exhibited by a defendant with autism include hand flapping or shifting the focus of the discussions to something that they want to talk about (for example, a specific preoccupation or special interest). Additionally, it can be extremely challenging to interrupt the individual and redirect them onto the topic or question of interest. During an investigative interview, such behaviour may be perceived as evasive, that is, that the individual may be attempting to hide something and are deliberately avoiding answering the questions the police have asked them. Again, this may infer guilt, with predictable consequences for the suspect. Organising and conveying information or thoughts when under stress can be particularly challenging for some autistic individuals, including difficulty in summarising or getting to the point (Allely, 2022). Even if an autistic individual remains 'on topic,' they may respond at significant length, with pedantic detail and in a repetitive manner (Allely & Cooper, 2017; Allely, 2022). This may also be interpreted as an individual's strategy for attempting to avoid addressing police questions directly, or as a method of hiding a needle in a haystack of irrelevant or tangential information.

Unusual Ways of Speaking

Autistic individuals frequently have unusual ways of speaking. For instance, they may suddenly and unexpectedly speak at an increased volume or at a very low volume. Sudden or unexpected utterances at very loud volumes by an autistic individual may automatically be perceived as being aggressive, rather than related to their diagnosis. Unusual or odd-sounding prosody is also common. For example, an individual may speak in a monotonous tone of voice, with no emotional intonation or variation in prosodic elements (for example, speech rate and rhythm, loudness, pitch/fundamental frequency, intensity, duration, and use of pause/silence) (McCann & Peppé, 2003). This can make police investigative interviewers view autistic individuals as cold or standoffish (Allely & Cooper, 2017).

Questioning an Autistic Individual: A Checklist of Useful Issues to Consider

Unlike a diagnostic interview, which has the aim of eliciting features of autism to support or exclude the diagnosis, other forensic interviews often have the aim of obtaining information from perpetrators, victims and witnesses regarding an alleged offence. In order to do this, Murphy (2018) developed a checklist of areas to be considered when interviewing an autistic individual in forensic settings, including possible appropriate adjustments and tips, which are likely to enhance the chances of obtaining more reliable information during an interview and minimise individual stress or anxiety. The checklist covers the following domains: personal safety, sensory issues, difficulties with reciprocal social communication, cognitive style and comorbidity.

Personal Safety

Depending on the circumstances and context, there may be a need to consider personal safety issues when interviewing some autistic individuals. Ideally, an interviewer would have access to any previously completed formal risk assessments and available case notes. In addition, it is often useful to speak with family members or members of staff who may have insight about any specific triggers to violence that the individual may have. If so, ensuring the interview is observed by an appropriate member of staff (for example, a nurse or other health practitioner) is recommended, as well as having a second person present and considering the seating arrangements and exit points in the interview room. As with all interviews, but especially so with someone with a very literal thinking style, there is the need to be explicit as to the purpose of the interview. In terms of interview duration, it may be better to have several short-duration interviews rather than a single extended one. For an individual with emotional regulation difficulties or poor frustration tolerance, such actions may significantly reduce the risk of them acting on any violent impulses. Another useful recommendation is for the interviewer to arrange the interview to take place at a time when it is unlikely to cause any disruption to an individual's routines or rituals.

Sensory Issues

Prior to interviews, the interviewer should seek information regarding any sensory functioning or any hypersensitivities that an individual may have, many of which may not be immediately obvious. Asking relatives or others who know the individual may be useful to obtain such information. Before an interview, asking the individual themselves if they have any sensory sensitivities can also be useful. For instance, asking them if anything in the room is causing them any discomfort (for example, fans, strip lights, direct eye contact) or interfering with their ability to focus on the interview. Selecting the interview for a particular time of day which is more quiet may also be useful (especially if an interview room is located in a busy area) to avoid times when there may be extra distractions such a noise. Asking the individual to complete a self-report measure such as the sensory profile checklist may also be useful. When first meeting an autistic individual, it is also recommended that any initial body contact is avoided (such as a handshake) unless the individual offers one and personal safety allows. Throughout the duration of the interview, an even and calm tone of voice should also be maintained by the interviewer. In some situations, allowing an individual to use a sensory aid (sometimes called 'stimming'; for example, letting an individual keep their hands busy by playing with a Tangle toy or a piece of cloth) can be helpful to keep an individual calm and anxiety levels contained (Salerno-Ferraro & Schuller, 2020).

Whilst most autistic individuals may be able to articulate their distress in response to sensory hypersensitivity, some individuals cannot and may experience an overload or 'sensory meltdown,' possibly leading to aggressive behaviour, a sensory shut down or reduced capacity to process information. As mentioned earlier, it is also possible that some individuals may cope with sensory overload by engaging in behaviours easily misinterpreted by a non-autism informed mind-set as being signs of avoidance or anti-social behaviours (for example, closing eyes, humming, rocking or swinging). In terms of direct eye contact by the interviewer, it is also possible that this may hinder an individual's capacity to answer questions or perform some tasks, including perhaps the recall of specific memories (Falck-Ytter et al., 2014). Although autistic individuals can vary significantly in their sensory profiles, it is wise for interviewers to be aware of how individuals might present when experiencing sensory overload (such as personal mannerisms and reactions), as well as what reasonable adjustments to the interview may be useful. Salerno-Ferraro and Schuller (2020) published a summary of recommendations that may be easily implemented by police officers and other law enforcement professionals when interacting with autistic individuals and also recommended that the professional(s) adopt a 'hands-off' approach when possible. This is due to the fact that touching an autistic individual may further escalate the situation and actually increase an autistic individual's sensory overload. During an initial encounter with an individual suspected as having autism on the streets or in the community, it is also recommended that any lights or sounds be turned off on a police vehicle.[3]

---

3 See Chapter 1.

Difficulties with Reciprocal Social Communication and Cognitive Style

Crucial to the interview process is an individual's capacity to engage with a reciprocal discussion, including the ability to understand and answer questions. Prior to an interview it is helpful for an interviewer to gather as much information as possible about an individual's ability to engage with a discussion, as well as any specific issues with comprehension and expression of language. For example, the interviewer could ask a parent or care provider for advice or perhaps to act as an intermediary during an interview. Such prior knowledge might allow planning as to how to conduct the interview and the questions to be asked, as well as the language to be used. For example, if an individual has particular difficulties with verbal communication or presents as electively mute, the use of a laptop or pen and notebook might be an option if this is their preferred method of answering questions. Although sometimes a slow process, this can be very useful in facilitating communication and judging an individual's literacy skills, as well as providing a written record of what was covered during the interview.

In terms of questions and language, particular planning and consideration may be required (Murphy, 2018, p. 315). For example, some autistic individuals may have difficulties with the pragmatic aspects of language. As mentioned earlier, they may interrupt when others are talking or have difficulties with engaging in a reciprocal dialogue, both of which can significantly restrict a meaningful exchange. In such cases, it can be helpful to outline to the individual at the beginning of the interview not only its purpose, but to clearly specify the start and finish times of the interview. The interviewer should also set out the 'rules' of discussion at the start of the interview such as no interrupting when others are talking and having a fixed length of time to talk (for example, two-minute intervals). However, there is also a need for interviewers to be mindful that many autistic individuals require additional time to process verbal information and to provide an answer to a question. In these circumstances, it is also important not to interrupt someone with autism when explaining something or to try to finish their sentences for them. Part of the prior planning of interviews should therefore include the expectation that it may take much longer to cover some information compared to someone without autism. A similar issue may also be present when administering any formal tasks such as questionnaires or self-report forms. Again, speaking with family, carers and teachers to help plan an interview and how best to communicate with an individual can also be helpful (Maras et al., 2018). This has previously been described in a number of sources, such as guidance provided by for advocates in England and Wales (The Advocate's Gateway, 2013). As discussed earlier, odd or inappropriate behaviours may become particularly observable when an autistic individual is feeling stressed or experiencing some form of sensory hypersensitivity. It is important that the interviewer is aware and understands how such behaviour is associated with autism and they do not interpret such behaviour to be indicative of them not taking the interview seriously.

In terms of the cognitive style of an individual, this may also have a significant impact on the interview process and it is wise for an interviewer to consider any previous information that might be available, such as neuropsychological assessments, which might inform the understanding of an individual's general intellectual functioning and cognitive style (for example, tendency towards literal thinking, issues with memory functioning) and also any vulnerability to suggestibility. In terms of the specific adaptations to questions, some general guidelines were recommended by Murphy (2018). Questions should be kept concise, and the individual should be given more time in order to process and comprehend questions and also given more time to provide answers. The interviewer should avoid questions which may be leading and ambiguous in interpretation. Questions should avoid the use of metaphor or sarcasm, and should avoid being non-literal and in need of some degree of inference, insinuation, deduction or abstractive extrapolation. Questions should be direct and avoid the use of 'tags' (for example, 'You went to the museum, didn't you?'). Negatives and double negatives should be avoided (for example, 'You would not disagree with that interpretation David, would you?' or 'Is it not the case that he did not go outside?'). As an unusual autobiographical memory is common in many autistic individuals, questions need to be framed in the correct tense and not make reference to a past event as if in the present (for example, 'Now you are in the street and looking at the house.'). Questions which consist of multiple parts should also be avoided (for example, 'On the morning of the 30th of January, were you in the park, and on the following morning did you see Aden?'). Questions which are phrased as statements should also be avoided, as such questions may not be recognised by someone with autism as something that can be disagreed with (for example, 'So, you saw him enter the house?'). Instead, this should be rephrased as a clear question (for example, 'Did you see him enter the house?').

Neurodevelopmental Disorder and Psychiatric Comorbidity

Another issue that would have a significant impact on obtaining an effective interview with someone who has autism is the presence of any co-occurring difficulties. Indeed, evidence suggests that additional neurodevelopmental disorders such as ADHD and intellectual difficulties, as well as mental health disorders, can also be common (Mahbub Hossain et al., 2020). For some, personality disorder, psychopathy and psychosis may also be present. Indeed, such difficulties may be particularly common among autistic individuals who have contact with the criminal justice system as perpetrators (Ghaziuddin et al., 1998; Gillberg & Billstedt, 2000; Im, 2016a, 2016b; Newman & Ghaziuddin, 2008; Wachtel & Shorter, 2013). When co-occurring difficulties are present or suspected in an individual, it may be necessary to seek additional assessments by suitably qualified professionals to determine their presence, including providing an opinion as to how it may influence an individual's presentation and perhaps capacity to engage with an interview. For example, it is often very difficult to disentangle what aspects of an individual's presentation may be linked to a personality disorder and what is linked to autism (Carthy & Murphy, 2021). In some circumstances the presence of positive symptoms associated with a psychosis, such as delusional ideas and hallucinations, can influence an individual's presentation during interview. Indeed, there is the suggestion that autistic individuals may be particularly vulnerable to acting on such symptoms (Wachtel & Shorter, 2013).

Autism and Police Knowledge, Training and Adaptations

The preceding discussions demonstrate the potential for autistic individuals to be drawn into the investigative process, to be vulnerable in this context and for negative outcomes to occur. This underlines the need for police officers to be aware of such issues and adapt accordingly. A number of studies which have highlighted deficits in this respect and the need for better formalised training on autism for police officers and other law enforcement professionals (discussed in Chapter 1; also see Gardner et al., 2019). Perhaps unsurprisingly, there is evidence that members of the autism community (such as parents and adults with autism) do not experience satisfying interactions with police (Crane et al., 2016; Helverschou et al., 2017). Using an online survey, Crane et al. (2016) sought experiences and views of autism from 394 police officers from England and Wales. One of the questions they asked the participants concerned the measures and adjustments they had used when interviewing someone with a diagnosis of autism (a total of 199 police officers responded to this question). The findings revealed that the adjustments that police made most commonly were avoiding long-winded or multiple-part questions (92%), allowing extra time to process questions (91%) and being mindful of the vocabulary used (89%). These adaptations showed some appreciation of autism and common challenges with communication and cognitive processing.

Another question asked participants how easy or difficult it was to make these adjustments (a total of 175 participants responded to this question; Crane et al., 2016). Nearly half (49%) of police officers reported it was easy to make these adjustments, with 19% saying they found it difficult (whilst 32 % were neutral). In 47 open-ended responses, officers expanded on why this was the case, specifically identifying time constraints and a lack of training as factors which were considered to be significant barriers to enabling them to make appropriate adaptations and adjustments to support autistic individuals in forensic interviews. Importantly, Crane and colleagues (2016) found that only 42% of officers were satisfied with how they had worked with autistic individuals. Although 37% of officers had received general training on autism, they identified a need for training which was tailored to specific policing roles (for example, frontline officers and detectives). As alluded to earlier, Crane et al. also explored the experiences of the autistic community (31 autistic adults, 49 parents), who were found to be largely dissatisfied with their experience of the police and also recommended the need for improved police training on autism. Deficits in training were also identified in a more recent pilot survey of 51 police officers in the US conducted by Christiansen et al. (2023). They found that 52.9% reported previous autism training, 34.8% reported personal experience with autism and 56.9% endorsed low overall knowledge of autism, perhaps reflecting some of limitations of any previous autism training.

The National Autistic Society (NAS)—along with different police forces—have also developed the use of Autism Alert Cards and autism 'passports' that an individual can have in their possession and which can be shown to others during difficult situations (such as an initial encounter with the police). The purpose of the Alert Card is to simply make police officers aware that an individual has autism, as well as giving key information such as the need to be patient, avoid physical contact, and possibly provide the name of an appropriate adult who can aid communication and provide support. In contrast, the passport is more personal and offers additional information on what reasonable adjustments may be helpful to meet a person's specific needs, as well as what additional physical health and medications they may need. The passport also includes a visual 'feeling thermometer' which can be shown to a police officer to further assist communication with a feeling that cannot be verbalised. Whilst there is currently general awareness training and recommendations provided by, for example, online training modules from the NAS, these are not mandatory. Although planned, but has yet to happen, in 2019 a police officer training bill for autism awareness was put forward (UK Parliament, 2019). The aim of this bill was to highlight what standard of autism awareness police forces needed to achieve and what good autism training should include (as well as seeking specific inclusion in the national policing curriculum for England and Wales), as well as what to expect of police officers with regard to their awareness and consideration of autism during their everyday duties.

Conclusion

Regardless as to whether an autistic individual is being interviewed as a witness, as a victim or as perpetrator of a crime, by failing to consider their specific difficulties and how they may impact on an interview—as well as not making some reasonable adjustments in how the interview is completed—is likely to result in a lack of meaningful information and undermine the reliability of any information later being used in court. As Maras et al. (2018) found, the use of non-literal and abstract language can result in inconsistencies in accounts provided by autistic individuals due to misunderstandings. Whilst a general mind-set that is sensitive to autism will lead to a more effective interview, it is also important to remember that every autistic individual should also be considered unique with regard to their presenting profile of cognitive, sensory sensitivities and emotional regulation characteristics, particularly so if co-occurring problems are present. As such, what works for one autistic individual may not necessarily work for another. As highlighted by Salerno-Ferraro and Scheuller (2020), if during an initial meeting an individual is suspected as having autism, then they should be asked about this and what things might be particularly difficult for them, as well as reminding them that they have the right to disclose any disabilities or mental health conditions.

3 Autistic Defendants in Court

Perceptions and Support for Accessing Justice

Clare Allely, Eddie Chaplin, Jody Salter,
Jane McCarthy and Felicity Gerry

Introduction

In 2006, the United Nations Special Rapporteur on Disability stated:

> People with developmental disabilities are particularly vulnerable to
> human rights violations. Also, people with disabilities are rarely taken
> into account, they have no political voice and are often a sub-group
> of already marginalised social groups, and therefore, have no power
> to influence governments. They encounter significant problems in
> accessing the judicial system to protect their rights or to seek remedies
> for violations, and their access to organizations that may protect their
> rights is generally limited.
>
> (United Nations, 2006)

More recently, in her report on the rights of persons with disabilities, the
United Nations (2019) asserted that the deprivation of liberty of disabled
persons was 'a major global human rights concern.' She highlighted that

> [p]ersons with disabilities are significantly overrepresented in
> mainstream settings of deprivation of liberty, such as prisons and
> immigration detention centres. While it is estimated that persons with
> disabilities represent 15 per cent of the population, in many countries
> the proportion of persons with disabilities in prisons represents as many
> as 50 per cent of prisoners.
>
> (United Nations, 2019)

As a result, a disproportionate number of disabled persons are 'invari-
ably placed into an extremely vulnerable position' (United Nations, 2019).
The United Nations (2019) argued that '[p]ersons with disabilities should
have access to justice on an equal basis with others to challenge any

DOI: 10.4324/9781003248774-4

deprivation of liberty.' To facilitate this—and generally promote protection of such vulnerable individuals—the report also asserted that '[s]tates must also promote appropriate training for those working in the field of the administration of justice.'

Autism Spectrum Disorders (ASDs) are neurodevelopmental disorders which are characterised by reciprocal social interaction and communication impairments, and restricted repetitive behaviours. The *Diagnostic and Statistical Manual of Mental Disorders, Fifth Edition* (*DSM-5*) characterises two core areas of impairment in ASD, namely, (1) 'persistent deficits in social communication and social interaction' and (2) 'restricted, repetitive patterns of behaviour, interests, or activities' (APA, 2013). Repetitive behaviours and restricted interests (RBRIs) characterise behaviours that can include motor movements, sensory reactions, rituals, routines and restricted interests. The same two categories are reflected in the *International Classification of Diseases and Related Health Problems, Eleventh Revision* (*ICD-11*; WHO, 2019). Both diagnostic manuals allow autism to be diagnosed alongside other conditions. The main difference is that the *ICD-11* gives guidance for distinguishing between autism with and without intellectual disability, whereas the *DSM-5* just acknowledges that they can co-occur. It is unknown what the true ASD prevalence is, but it is commonly considered to occur in about 1% of the general population.

As recognised developmental disabilities, ASDs should be approached as such in the context of the criminal justice system. There is a growing body of literature which has established that individuals with ASDs[1] are significantly disadvantaged throughout the criminal justice system (CJS) (Cooper et al., 2022; Gormley et al., 2021; Slavny-Cross et al., 2022). Research suggests that the degree of vulnerability is evident across the entirety of the CJS, beginning with initial interactions with police (Haas and Gibbs, 2021), the police interview (Hepworth, 2017; Murphy et al., 2018), the courtroom—consequently impacting both juror verdicts and judges' sentencing (Allely et al., 2018; Berryessa, 2015; Maras et al., 2019)—and subsequently within the prison environment (Allely, 2015; Allely et al., 2022;

---

1 The use of identity-first language—'autistic people'—is seen by some as a way of highlighting autism as a part of a person's identity and as a way of being, rather than a focus on the medicalised concept of a 'disorder' (Kenny et al., 2016, p. 443). A study carried out in the UK found the endorsement of the term 'autistic' by a large percentage of autistic adults and family/friends. Findings also showed that professionals were more likely to endorse person-first language (e.g., 'person with autism'). Interestingly, the findings from a study carried out in Australia indicated that there was a preference for person-first language by individuals who reported a diagnosis of ASD (Bury et al., 2020). From hereon we use 'individuals with ASD.'

Newman et al., 2019). In response to academic findings and anecdotal evidence, a UK government inspection examined neurodiversity in the CJS, including ASD, and identified 'serious gaps, failings and missed opportunities' (CJJI, 2021). Consistent with academic findings, the report concluded that 'fair treatment, fair outcomes and equal access are currently not being achieved for all neurodivergent individuals' (CJJI, 2021).

Such findings raise fundamental questions regarding the effectiveness of current provisions within the CJS and challenges the core principle of the rule of law if justice is not equally accessible to all. This chapter serves as both a summary and exploration of the theme that criminal courts—in terms of functions and processes—are not autism-friendly, and that they take insufficient account of autistic defendants' needs. As a result, this not only leads to a negative experience for defendants but also places them at a disadvantage within our adversarial system, undermining their fair-trial rights. This chapter outlines how certain features of ASD may be perceived negatively in the courtroom by criminal justice professionals and decision makers. Additionally, the chapter considers—using two case studies—various issues related to substantive evidence in criminal trials, examining the importance of decision makers (and expert witnesses) fully understanding and considering ASD when determining the intention, understanding or complicity of a defendant. The chapter concludes by discussing the role of Liaison and Diversion (L&D) services in the early identification within police stations and their role in supporting defendants with ASD through the court system recognising the importance of specific expertise being available for clinical assessments to advise the court on appropriate disposal options.

ASD and the Right to a Fair Trial

Individuals with ASD are commonly referred to as being on a spectrum, ranging from severely impaired to mildly impaired. There is a need to move away from this misconception.[2] It is more accurate to consider that each individual with ASD has a profile which includes both strengths and weaknesses. This is important as many individuals with ASD who are said to be 'high functioning' who become involved in the CJS are at significant risk of not receiving a fair trial. This is because it is not appreciated or understood that even though they are high functioning, they still have significant impairments that might not be so immediately apparent (for example, not as obvious as impaired social interaction abilities). Having

2 See discussion in Chapter 2.

high-functioning ASD should not automatically negate the fact that a defendant may have impairments that may be important to consider, both in terms of understanding how it might relate to their offending, and/or how they may present during court proceedings. A diagnosis of ASD, regardless of the defendant's level of functioning, should never automatically be considered immaterial to their defence. Strengths in many high-functioning individuals with ASD can mask other impairments or weaknesses that they may have and may make them appear to be relatively unimpaired— particularly in individuals who have a limited understanding of ASD. Terms which are commonly used in forensic contexts such as 'mildly autistic,' high-functioning autism (without further expansion) and 'mild autism' are unhelpful and potentially detrimental to the potential for an individual with ASD to receive a fair trial (Allely, 2022). The fact that an individual with ASD appears to socially engage and understand does not automatically mean that they truly appreciate the specific circumstances of the situation they are in (Berryessa, 2021); their response to their context may be considerably more nuanced (Freckelton, 2021). Because of this appearance of understanding in some individuals with ASD, it can be a significant challenge to identify an individual with ASD (Dickie et al., 2018).

The right to a fair trial is a fundamental human right for all those accused of criminal offences, enshrined in English and Welsh law under the Human Rights Act 1998. It is imperative that everyone has the right to a fair trial operationalised in a way which assesses for all possible contributing factors, irrespective of any condition which may have affected their criminal conduct (Allely, 2022). It is also imperative that ASD is identified and taken into consideration as early as possible during the criminal justice process (see Cooper & Allely, 2017, which discusses the evolving professional responsibilities, liabilities and 'judgecraft' when a party has an ASD). As part of this, there are three areas that need to be considered: how the individual presents, how the process may need to be adapted to enable the defendant to effectively participate, and how the disability may affect the legal and factual issues in the trial.

When a defendant has a disability and adaptations are made in court, it is expected that a magistrate will accept (or a jury will be directed to accept) that the person needs those adaptations but without giving details as to the person's condition. This now forms part of the approach to equal treatment (Equal Treatment Bench Book, 2021). The idea is to ensure that the decisions to be made on the issues are not affected by assumptions or prejudice as to conditions. However, it has been raised that when the magistrate or jury (hereafter the 'decision maker') is not provided with information regarding the defendant's diagnosis of ASD, they are left to assume that the defendant is unimpaired (Foster, 2015). Foster (2015) has argued that not providing information regarding the defendant's ASD may *increase* levels of confusion in jurors because many of the social mannerisms, expressions and behaviours which individuals with ASD often exhibit are similar to those observed by a guilty party. Bias amongst magistrates or judges in this respect has not been measured. This tends to suggest that courts should ensure that decision makers understand any disability and are educated not to make biased assumptions.

Allely (2022) has recommended that if the defendant's ASD diagnosis is explained to the jury, any expert witness should avoid words and phrases such as 'a neuro-developmental condition,' 'social interaction impairment,' 'unusually intense and circumscribed interests,' 'mild Asperger's condition' or 'high-functioning autism.' Such descriptions or explanations regarding ASD are unlikely to be helpful to the court unless they are explained in detail and related directly to the defendant and their offending and/or presentation during court proceedings. For instance, based on a case-by-case approach, the expert provides the court with information pertaining directly to how the defendant's particular features of ASD may have provided the context of vulnerability to their offence(s) (Allely, 2022). When individuals with ASD are charged with an offence, in addition to assessing what adaptations that person may need to effectively participate in the trial process, there needs to be consideration of whether their features of ASD may have provided the context of vulnerability to engaging in alleged offending behaviour. It can be a real challenge for criminal justice professionals to always quickly identify an individual with ASD given its heterogeneity (King & Murphy, 2014). No two individuals are the same in terms of their ASD profile (which includes both strengths and weakness as mentioned earlier). What can further complicate identification is the high likelihood of co-occurring mental health conditions or other neurodevelopmental disorders such as attention deficit hyperactivity disorder (ADHD). A diagnosis of 'pure' ASD (ASD by itself) is the exception and not the norm (Gillberg and Billstedt, 2000).

ASDs and Procedural Rights: Presentation and Effective Participation

Certain features of ASD may be perceived negatively in the courtroom by criminal justice professionals and decision makers. For example, in the case of *R v Sultan* [2008], the court provided a direction to explain why an autistic defendant was reading a book during the trial. At present there is no system to measure whether such directions function to increase or decrease bias. In addition, because of certain features of their ASD, a defendant can be perceived as being evasive, remorseless, lacking in empathy and guilty

(Allely, 2022). Cea (2014) discussed a hypothetical case of a male defendant with a diagnosis of ASD being prosecuted for assault and battery. Although hypothetical, the context and features described are common. Crucially, the case serves to highlight the significant risk that the demeanour of a defendant with ASD during court proceedings will be perceived negatively by judges, decision makers and other criminal justice professionals—even amongst the defence team. Cea describes the male defendant as nervous-looking and barely reacting on the stand. He is also described as displaying no emotional expression (such as shock) when shown a picture which depicts the woman's injuries because of an assault and battery. There are no stereotypical signs of any remorse by the defendant, for instance, he does not state that he is sorry for his actions. The jury takes a dislike to this defendant because they do not understand why he is not exhibiting any emotion. The defendant pleaded guilty, and during the sentencing hearing leniency was sought. When the judge asks the defendant if he understands that his actions were wrong, he simply shrugs in response. The judge gives the defendant the maximum sentence believing that he was not willing to take any responsibility for his offending (Cea, 2014).

As already mentioned, there exists a range of features of ASD that a defendant with this diagnosis can exhibit during court proceedings that can make them be perceived as aloof, disinterested, remorseless or even impervious to decision makers who may not be familiar with the disorder (O'Sullivan, 2018). Even if professionals and decision makers are familiar with ASD (for instance, through personal experience or training), because no two individuals with ASD are the same, they may fail to understand why the ASD defendant is presenting in a way that contrasts with their personal experience or training.

Very often, ASD individuals are impaired in their ability to appreciate the subjective experiences of other people (commonly referred to as theory of mind [ToM]).[3] Given that individuals with ASD are frequently impaired in their ability to appreciate the subjective experiences of others, they may not exhibit any outward expressions of empathy, which can lead observers to make the (quite natural) assumption that individuals with ASD are cold, calculating, arrogant or remorseless; in a court context this can have devastating outcomes (Archer & Hurley, 2013; Allely & Cooper, 2017). However, it is important to understand that many individuals with ASD may display no emotional expression, but this does not necessarily reflect what they feel internally (Allely & Cooper, 2017). Additionally, some of their facial expressions can also be considered awkward or inappropriate. For

3 See Chapter 2.

example, during court proceedings, an autistic defendant may start laughing suddenly when the alleged victim is being questioned (Allely, 2022). Again, such outward expressions are not necessarily reflective of internal thoughts and feelings (Allely & Cooper, 2017).

Many individuals with ASD can have an odd or pedantic manner of speaking. They may, irrespective of how innocuous or not the topic of conversation is, unexpectedly speak at an increased volume or very low volume and also unexpectedly shout out unrelated words or phrases, which can often cause others to consider them rude or even aggressive or angry (even though this might not be the case or reflective of what they are feeling internally). Also, many individuals with ASD can exhibit an unusual or odd-sound prosody and speak in a monotonous voice, with no emotional intonation or no variation in prosodic elements (for example, speech rate and rhythm, loudness, intensity; McCann & Peppé, 2003). Such presentation would most likely be considered cold or standoffish, with obvious negative implications in a court context (Allely and Cooper, 2017). During the court proceedings, they may also misinterpret or 'nit-pick' questions that are posed to them during cross-examination (Berryessa, 2021). As previously described by Freckelton and List (2009), 'the language of persons with Asperger's can be eccentric, tangential, formal, and easily capable of misinterpretation,' which can be viewed negatively, particularly within a forensic context. For instance, a defendant may appear to be evasive if they are asked a question and then do not answer the question but instead talk about something that they think is important or relates to their restricted interests (Allely, 2022).

Additionally, when being questioned in court, many autistic individuals can exhibit marked weaknesses in mental processing speed. When they are asked a question, many individuals with ASD require additional time to allow them to process verbal information and formulate an answer due to difficulty processing linguistic and social information (Crane & Maras, 2018; Murphy, 2018). This additional time which is needed by some individuals with ASD is frequently referred to as 'Asperger time' (Jacobsen, 2003; Myles et al., 2005). As such, defendants would frequently need more time to respond to questions, particularly if they are asked very rapidly or unexpectedly (Kroncke et al., 2016), and irrespective of whether the person is high functioning or not. Consideration also needs to be made regarding how many individuals with ASD will attempt to cope with the overstimulatory nature of the court proceedings (such as rapid firing of questions) by narrowing their focus to a certain aspect of what is happening. This coping behaviour by some individuals with ASD may lead them to fail to identify some broader issues contained within the questioning or miss out on key details going on around them. Therefore, they are not effectively participating in their trial as a result.

Individuals with ASD can also experience significant difficulty with making and/or maintaining eye contact (known as 'gaze avoidance'). This can make the individual appear to decision makers as rude, unconcerned with court proceedings or even guilty. For example, a defendant with ASD may look down at the table in front of them, which may lead the court (professionals and decision makers) to draw negative conclusions (Allely, 2022). If not understood fully within the context of ASD, this can be viewed as evidence of shame or guilt, based on the belief that they are unable to even look their alleged victim(s) or anyone else (including decision makers) in the eye. However, many individuals with ASD do this as a form of coping strategy, by minimising the amount of stimulation and sensory overload they are experiencing (Allely & Cooper, 2017).

The social communication impairments that individuals with ASD exhibit may impede their ability to appear likeable to professionals or decision makers (Grant et al., 2018). They may also find it difficult to recognise simple conventions in conversation and appear rude as a result. For example, they may start talking before the professional has finished asking a question because they are unable to identify or recognise social cues which are used to signal the end of a conversation. They may also make comments to others that appear to be tactless, or they may be brutally honest (Taylor et al., 2009). There may also have an impaired ability to recollect or remember past personally experienced events and remember fewer of them. Remembering or recollecting past personally experienced events may also take individuals with ASD longer compared with individuals who do not have an ASD (Goddard et al., 2007; Crane et al., 2012). Individuals with ASD have also been found to often be impaired in their ability to recall events in a sequential manner (Kroncke et al., 2016). Lastly, some individuals with ASD can appear as arrogant and rude as they can sometimes be quite blunt in their responses to questions, which may be due to their literal cognitive style or interpretation of information (Murphy, 2018). All of the above can have negative implications in a court context, for not only their access to proceedings, but for decisions and outcomes about them.

In summary, it is vital for all involved in court processes to understand the behavioural characteristics of ASD in order to reduce the negative impact this could have on the defendant, in terms of how their behaviour is interpreted and responded to. There are a range of special measures that are available for vulnerable witnesses (Youth Justice and Criminal Evidence Act [YJCEA], 1999); in rare cases, such measures can be made available for defendants or—outside of the legislative framework—at the discretion of the court. Adaptations might include reducing the number of people in court, allowing the defendant to sit outside of the dock and with a family member, or to have the assistance of an intermediary to assist with communication. However, there is currently no available data on how often such measures are used for defendants nor how effective they are. In those jurisdictions where special measures and adaptations have been legislated for victims and witnesses, these should not be limited for accused persons. Advocates should seek to educate the court on their client's traits or needs and seek reasonable adaptations (even if it involves using a court's inherent discretion) as an issue of procedural fairness. Research suggests a more holistic approach to 'trauma-informed' courts would be preferable to measures for a specific category of stakeholder (such as witnesses) and that a trauma-informed approach is integral to the integrity of the court process (Gerry, 2021).

ASDs and Alleged Offending: Evidence of Culpability versus Evidence of Vulnerability

Research indicates that when an individual with ASD does offend, they may be more likely to engage in specific crimes, such as violent conduct, threatening behaviour and damage to property (Allen et al., 2008; Robinson et al., 2012). Notably, epidemiological studies have concluded that ASD does not increase a person's likelihood of committing violent crime once other factors, such as comorbid diagnoses and life circumstances, have been taken into account. However, there is a danger that behaviour by an individual with ASD is seen as an increased risk and thus greater culpability, rather than considered in the context of disability. Two particular offending contexts give rise to concerns: radicalised terrorist offending and offending as a secondary party. On the first, it is important to note here that there is no evidence to suggest that individuals with ASD are at an increased risk of radicalisation (Allely, 2022; Faccini et al., 2017). However, it has been recognised that risk factors inherent to ASD such as the intensity of circumscribed interests and cognitive rigidity, combined with impairments to social communication may play a role in facilitating the pathway towards radicalisation (Allely, 2022; Faccini et al., 2017). Therefore, when individuals with ASD become involved in allegations of serious offending—such as preparing, planning or executing acts of terrorism—it is crucial to assess the complex interplay between the core features of ASD and radicalisation.

On the second, the failure to fully consider ASD in the context of disability causes three concerns in cases where an individual is accused of committing a crime as a secondary party: first, the extent to which the individual knows what others would do; second, the extent to which the past record of an individual with ASD is used as evidence of bad character rather than as evidence of disability; and third, whether the individual can truly be regarded as being as culpable as the principal offender. There is limited research in relation to individuals with ASD and complicity crimes, that is, playing a secondary role in a plan or as an accessory to a crime. Traditionally, complicity requires *knowledge* of essential facts and acts, which demonstrates an intention to agree to, assist or encourage a particular crime. Various issues might be explored, for example, the extent to which such individuals may know and understand the essential terms of such a plan or act intentionally in furtherance of someone else's crime (especially when events may be spontaneous and agreement to a plan is alleged to be 'tacit'). There is a reluctance by courts to recognise ASD as negating the ability to intend to agree or assist, because this risks defining individuals with ASD as lacking capacity or suffering with insanity, legal definitions which have been developed in relation to people with mental health issues rather than ASD features. However, there is a risk of an assumption of complicity, particularly in group-based violent crime when young people are alleged to have acted as a team. It can be difficult for individuals with ASDs to assess and predict the conduct of others; as such, their conduct and state of mind can be misconstrued as intentional or reckless, when it is not.

Case Study: Paul Dunleavy v R [2021] EWCA Crim 39

In August 2019, 16-year-old Paul Dunleavy (PD) was arrested by West Midlands Police, West Midlands Counter Terrorism Unit (WMCTU). Following a search of his bedroom, police found a handgun, air rifle, shotgun cartridges, bullet casings, several knives, and a notebook containing swastikas and details of 'lone wolf' terror attacks. Phone analysis discovered over 90 documents containing information on firearms and explosives, including evidence of extreme right-wing ideology (Warwickshire Police, 2020), suggesting membership to the extremist group Feuerkrieg Division (FDK), a neo-Nazi organisation advocating violence and terrorism to incite a race war (NPCC, 2020). PD, at age 17, was charged with and pleaded not guilty to various terrorism-related offences under the Terrorism Acts of 2000 and 2006. He was found guilty by a jury, and sentenced to 7.5 years in custody. PD was subsequently was diagnosed with ASD by a forensic psychologist, whose report formed the basis of an appeal against his conviction.

Among the issues at the basis of the appeal was PD's 'obsessive and compulsive pursuit of information about guns,' which could be regarded as a presentation of his ASD, as opposed to offending behaviour. This was, however, not accompanied by any particularly detailed analysis of this particular obsession; unsurprisingly, this contention was rejected by the Court of Appeal. This deficit arguably increased the risk of an unfair outcome; indeed, it is likely that PD's diagnosis of ASD could in part explain his intense interest in weaponry rather than as a result of offending behaviour (see Al-Attar, 2018, 2020; Allely, 2022). However, without further investigation, such as detailed interviews with PD, this cannot be fully understood and the default assumption—that is, offending behaviour—becomes the primary explanation. Similarly, another aspect of the appeal that was rejected due to insufficient exploration by an expert was the suggestion that PD did not anticipate that any messages posted online would be acted upon by others due to ToM mind deficits—particularly a lack of appreciation of the intentions and desires of others. As such, the argument was that his behaviour was a result of social naivety arising from ASD, as opposed to intentional offending behaviour. Despite general evidence to suggest a link between ToM and acts of violence (Lerner et al., 2012) and, arguably, a fundamental issue to this appeal, the failure to address this fully was detrimental.

Alongside these issues of evidence, the appeal also raised the possible impact on the jury of PD's matter-of-fact responses (as they were suggested to be) to questions in cross-examination (as discussed earlier). Additionally, it was argued that PD incriminated himself on the stand, leaving him no choice but to plead guilty to several counts. The tendency to 'self-incriminate' during questioning is not uncommon for those with ASD (Allely, 2015; Hepworth, 2017; O'Sullivan, 2018). Again, these arguments were rejected. The court highlighted that the psychologist did not see the defendant give evidence, nor commented on the way PD gave evidence, concluding that 'there was no evidence his ASD could have affected the way he gave his account' (though it is arguable that it may have not been necessary for the psychologist to observe PD giving evidence to explain his matter-of-fact responses).

Finally, it was also argued that PD's behaviour could be explained by engagement in 'fantasy' behaviour in an online context and its difference to intentional offending behaviour, with the argument that individuals with ASD have difficulty distinguishing between the two. Impairments in this context have been described in relation to both cybercrimes and radicalisation (Allely, 2022). Al-Attar (2020) describes how sharing information of terroristic fantasy by those with ASD may not always be suggestive of meaningful intent nor increased risk of acting out the fantasy. However, as with the other grounds of appeal, there was an absence of evidence to address this issue, with the court stating that the psychologist 'had not suggested that the applicant or others with ASD suffer from delusional fantasies.' A detailed assessment of PD would have been critical in establishing the fantasy element. Clinicians are advised to assess the role of terroristic fantasy with accompanying compulsions and addictive features, including personal triggers (Al-Attar, 2020).

Case Study: **Alex Henry v R**

In *Alex Henry v R*, the accused was convicted as an accessory to murder on the basis that he joined in a fight in which someone died. The jury did not know he had an ASD as he was diagnosed post-conviction; however, the Court of Appeal (dismissing his challenge against conviction) refused to receive expert evidence, rejecting the diagnosis and accusing his mother of assisting the appellant to fake symptoms. Had the court accepted the diagnosis (which was confirmed post-appeal), the evidence would arguably have been relevant. Such evidence would have enabled a decision maker to understand the effect of an ASD on the individual's ability to understand the intentions of others and make choices about their own behaviour. Had the court accepted the diagnosis (which was confirmed post-appeal), the evidence would arguably have been relevant due to several common features of ASD, including social naiveté (leading to manipulation), communication difficulties (leading to failures to consult others about how to solve a problem or misunderstanding meaning), obsessive thinking (leading to an inability to let go of a proposed plan), heightened anxiety (leading panic-based, extreme actions), executive dysfunction (leading to overfocusing on one detail and not considering longer-term consequences of actions), and ToM difficulties (leading to challenges imagining a victim's perspective).

Such evidence—explored in a detailed manner—would have enabled a decision maker to understand the effect of an ASD on the individual's ability to understand the intentions of others and make choices about their own behaviour. This is vital in the context of complicity. In a study by Berryessa (2014), it was found that judges struggled to 'completely understand the roles of and abilities of these offenders to formulate intent … and how to consider it in their rulings.' She concluded that questions might be asked about 'whether [such] offenders are exculpable from their actions because they are unable to exhibit the essential elements of a crime.' Those with ASDs suffer a significant disadvantage if their ASD and its effects are not understood in the trial process. Accordingly, it becomes increasingly necessary for decision makers to understand the individual's disability.

These case studies demonstrate the importance of detailed and knowledgeable examination—prior to trial and certainly prior to appeal—of issues such as compulsion, obsession, ToM, and social communication issues, and their relationship to alleged offending behaviour. However, at present, reliance on psychological reports may in fact increase the vulnerability of defendants with ASD. Research has shown that two-thirds of psychological reports submitted to family courts were rated as 'below the expected standard,' highlighting the urgent need for quality control (Ireland et al., 2012). Indeed, in *Dunleavy*, the court critiqued the report for a 'lack of specificity' and 'general lack of analysis,' which were 'fatal to the appeal.' Indeed, the evidence suggests that the forensic psychologist did not possess the necessary expertise in ASD to sufficiently assist the court (Gerry & Cooper, 2017).

ASD and L&D

L&D services in both police stations and courts have been developed to identify and support vulnerable defendants. This includes those who present with mental health and/or substance misuse issues, or with a neurodevelopmental disorder (NDD) such as intellectual disability (ID), ADHD and ASD. To date there has been limited research on defendants with ASD in courts, which has predominantly focused on severe mental illness and substance use. The lack of attention to ASD makes prevalence estimates difficult to establish given issues of identifying new cases and a lack of robust epidemiological studies into L&D populations (Chaplin et al., 2021a, 2021b). Currently, the assessment of ASD varies considerably across L&D services; it is largely dependent upon the availability of specific expertise and local policy arrangements, and hindered by a lack of screening and diagnostic services related to ASD.

Identification, Assessment and Advice to the Court

Individuals brought to court or into police custody, who are deemed vulnerable will be referred to the L&D team. However, with reliable screening and identification of ASD yet to be developed and implemented in many cases, it is likely to continue to be missed. In terms of screening, the National Institute for Health and Care Excellence (NICE) guidelines recommend the Autism Spectrum Quotient (AQ-10) (Wilson et al., 2014) be used to screen for autism, and though this was developed using community samples, it has been adopted in various clinical and criminal justice settings. Early research within the CJS suggests that this instrument has limitations as it can be over-inclusive, often identifying autistic traits in people who do not present with an ASD (McCarthy et al., 2015). Screening tools may also be problematic to administer within a court environment. The use of diagnostic instruments such as the Autism Diagnostic Observation Schedule–Generic (ADOS-G) (Lord, 2000) and the Autism Diagnostic Interview–Revised (ADI-R) (Lord et al., 1997) following screening are rarely or never used due to time and capacity constraints of court staff. Instead, they will usually be conducted via specialist assessment later in the process.

As discussed earlier, the identification of ASD allows accurate reports to be provided to courts that may provide information on risk, presentation, understanding and mitigation as the court directs, enabling more effective decisions and adjustments to promote fair trials. Increasingly, information is requested from nursing staff or voluntary sector providers, in more complex cases, as are psychiatric reports, which can either be provided as part of the L&D service or via the instruction of an expert witness, and can be requested by the defence or the prosecution or the court itself. Any assessments or subsequent recommendations for defendants with ASD will usually include a mental state examination to take into account the key presenting symptoms and core deficits (for example, social communication, interaction and restrictive interests) and to consider their role, if any, in alleged offending behaviour. This is the starting point for clinicians to understand any relationship between ASD and offences. Many defendants with ASD will have more insight into what causes them to behave in such a way than is credited to them. Studies examining triggers to their behaviour have reported that some with ASD will recognise some change in themselves or circumstances such as reporting feelings of stress and excitement (Helverschou et al., 2015) or being upset, agitated, having bad habits, being impulsive, family or work problems, or having mental health problems (Allen et al., 2008). Given the importance and impact such reports can have—as demonstrated in *Dunleavy* and *Henry*—a practitioner interviewing someone with an ASD for the purposes of a legal report needs knowledge of the condition and how this influences future risk, and what might be done to mitigate this.

To improve the reliability and validity of an interview, several things should be considered to ensure reasonable adjustments such as the ability of the individual to understand and cope with the requirements of the court process; whether behaviours associated with ASD are present which might be misinterpreted by others; whether the individual is overcompliant with the process or inhibited by the situation, place and/or authority; and whether there are neuropsychiatric problems, including impaired motor, cognitive, social and communication functioning. In terms of supporting defendants with ASD, it has been reported that lawyers were 7.58 times more likely to have concerns about the effective participation of autistic defendants in court and were nearly four times more likely to be concerned about the risk of self-harm compared to non-autistic defendants (Slavny-Cross et al., 2022). Three-quarters of autistic defendants did not receive any reasonable adjustments, with less than half receiving an appropriate adult at the police stage. With lawyers reporting that they did not have an adequate understanding of autism (Slavny-Cross et al., 2022).

Comorbidities

Advances in health, social care and the criminal justice services to support offenders with NDD are now of international interest (Hollomotz & Talbot, 2021).

A study of three jurisdictions—New South Wales in Australia; Norway; and England and Wales—found all had a process for supporting vulnerable defendants (McCarthy et al., 2021). However, to date, there is still no explicit pathway for defendants with an ASD, though a new service specialising in neurodevelopmental conditions has been developed at a London Magistrates Court which integrates a specialist NDD service in parallel to the existing Court Mental Health L&D service (as described in Chaplin et al., 2021b). In a forthcoming study of five London courts, 9088 referrals to L&D services reported a rate of 1.1% of defendants with an ASD, with the most common comorbidity being ID (6.5%). Overall, defendants with NDD were younger, while women were less likely than others to be diagnosed with an ND. Accurate diagnosis has implications for treatment, whereas misdiagnosis of any primary or comorbid ND such as ASD can serve to complicate and misinform any intervention strategy or indeed the approach to court processes and adjudication. The interface between mental health issues and a defendant with ASD is also poorly understood yet impactful. Estimates of attempted suicide suggest those with an ASD are over nine times more likely than in the general population (Cassidy et al., 2014). Another study reported on prisoners screening positive with autistic traits, who were also significantly more likely to report having attempted suicide during their lifetime compared to non-autistic prisoners (64.9% compared to 11.6%) (Chaplin et al., 2021a). Although an area of concern and underexplored, it is now receiving more attention which will further understanding (Cassidy et al., 2020b, 2020a).

Moving Forward

There is now evidence that specialist services aimed at NDDs can successfully integrate with existing L&D services, as seen with other groups of vulnerable defendants (Forrester et al., 2020), and has highlighted a need for specialist staff or specific L&D services for people with ASD. This is necessary not only to achieve clinical excellence and best practice, but to bring genuine equity for people with ASD who proceed through court processes. It is still the case that many individuals appearing before L&D services may not be known to have an ASD, and a move towards a more inclusive model offers an opportunity to identify ASD and advise the court on features that may impact many of the problems highlighted in this chapter. Such information clearly has implications for case preparation, trials and sentencing. More restrictive approaches are inevitably facilitated by a lack of understanding and awareness amongst CJS professionals (including L&D), which in turn can cause communication misunderstandings and unfair outcomes. The use of expertise in ASD within L&D services is necessary for the early identification of unknown ASD, as well as other mental health and unmet general health needs. Earlier detection allows the signposting and onward referral of individuals to support from community-based services much earlier. This will ultimately improve health, social and justice outcomes—particularly in the context of court proceedings.

Conclusions

This chapter has offered a general overview of how individuals with ASD can be significantly disadvantaged in the context of the criminal courts. A generalised approach to ASD as a clinical disorder, both in terms of addressing individuals' needs and preferences and creating awareness in the CJS, may not be useful. For example, the use of clinical or legal language such as 'a neurodevelopmental condition' or 'unusually intense and circumscribed interests' will mean little unless explained in detail using plain language. Essential is a case-by-case approach, where the information relates to an individual's particular features of ASD that may show vulnerability or may be mitigating factors to their offence(s). This should also offer context to the individual's engagement and understanding. One particular issue for those who come across as able to engage or described as high functioning is that this may mask significant impairments that may not be immediately apparent and as a result overlooked particularly by those who have a limited understanding of ASD.

In several court cases the decision not to include evidence of psychiatric or psychological experts has been made, reasoning that any probative value would be substantially outweighed by the potential of confusing the jury. However, not providing information on a defendant's diagnosis of ASD may lead to the assumption that the defendant is unimpaired and may increase confusion as jurors try to interpret any social mannerisms, expressions and behaviours that may be mistaken for guilt, or as being evasive, remorseless or lacking in empathy. These issues are illustrated in the chapter using real and hypothetical case studies which dissect the issues in practice to provide understanding and context. This is to help understand the behavioural characteristics of ASD in the court environment to reduce the negative impact and reduce the risk of misinterpretation in the criminal justice system.

With no agreed L&D models for autistic defendants, pathway development is in its infancy, and more discussion is needed on how L&D services are offered and the essential components required for provision for autistic defendants to be integrated into existing systems and pathways. As well as improving general awareness, bespoke training programmes are needed to allow different professions to be able to understand the information in the context of the individual. Consideration also needs to be given to reasonable adjustments to benefit the autistic defendant. This could be cost-effective as it may also meet the need of neurotypical defendants and others who may benefit from new approaches. For example, making the environment less stimulating or adding quiet spaces so as not to inadvertently increase arousal levels is likely to benefit all defendants.

To properly accommodate an individual with ASD would move the CJS from a binary model of conduct and fault to a more comprehensive assessment of the individual and the alleged crime. A total change to a psychological evaluation of every accused could be as unbalanced as a system that admits no evidence of ASD. Some steps have been made in the procedural context. There is greater reluctance to change the approach to substantive issues of guilt or innocence. With no agreed models and pathway development in its infancy, more discussion is needed on how the CJS approaches accused individuals with ASD, and how L&D services for defendants with ASDs are offered, and what are the essential components required for provision to be integrated into existing systems and pathways.

Increased awareness through training and exposure to this group of accused persons can inform reasonable adjustments that will not only benefit autistic defendants but others who may have needs that will benefit from new approaches. It may also be helpful to understand whether the person is truly criminally culpable or acting in consequence of a condition which has not been understood and may be manageable. This in turn allows for crime prevention by potentially reducing recidivism, as an individual with ASD can learn to cope with their condition. Procedurally, making the environment less stimulating or adding quiet spaces so not to inadvertently increase arousal levels is a small but useful step; choosing not to criminalise individuals with ASD will be a much greater leap. In the meantime, this chapter seeks to improve general awareness and to emphasise the need for bespoke training programmes. The important approach is to ensure professionals and decision makers are able to understand the information in the context of the individual and to apply that knowledge in a fair way to the allegations.

4 Autism in Prisons

An Overview of Experiences of
Custody and Implications for
Custodial Rehabilitation for Autistic
Prisoners

Luke P Vinter and Gayle Dillon

Introduction

The core characteristics of autism are well documented elsewhere in this book and so are not outlined extensively here. Rather, what this chapter invites readers to do is to consider autism and the challenges faced by autistic individuals[1] in prison settings through a social model lens. A significant amount of literature on autism is dominated by the medical model which regards and documents autism as an inherent disorder (that is, Autism Spectrum Disorder, or ASD), manifesting as a cluster of symptoms or traits that can be used to diagnose an individual, for example, 'persistent deficits in social communication and social interaction' and 'restricted, repetitive patterns of behavior, interests, or activities' (APA, 2013, p. 50). Through this model, the challenges or limitations that autistic individuals experience are often regarded as intrinsically linked to, and a direct result of, an individual's autism (see Figure 4.1). As such, interventions and management strategies that fall within this framework will aim to address an individual's autism, providing ways to address or ameliorate the impact of perceived deficits.

However, for the purpose of this chapter, the authors take an alternative perspective: the social model view. Through this perspective, whilst it is recognised that autistic individuals may think, behave and experience

---

1 Note on language: For the purposes of this chapter, identity-first language (i.e., autistic individual) is used throughout, rather than a person-first approach (i.e., person with autism). This was a conscious decision made with a view to reflect the expressed views of the autistic community (see Bottema-Beutel et al., 2021, and Kenny et al., 2016). Nonetheless, the authors recognise that this preference is not ubiquitously held across the entire autistic community, and that individual preferences can vary and should be respected.

DOI: 10.4324/9781003248774-5

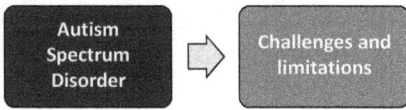

Figure 4.1 Medical model view of autism.

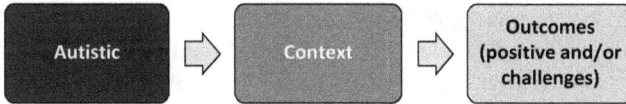

Figure 4.2 Social model view of autism.

the world in a way unique to neurotypical individuals,[2] it is suggested that challenges or positive outcomes an autistic individual faces are intrinsically linked to context (see Figure 4.2). That is, often, an autistic individual may experience challenges or flourish according to the context around them, as opposed to being an inevitable consequence of their autistic traits. Therefore, through this perspective, support and management strategies are best directed towards the context surrounding an autistic individual, as opposed to solely focusing on an individual's autistic traits.

As a consequence, for the purposes of this chapter, discussions will centre on how, and whether, a prison can be a challenging or supportive context for autistic individuals who have been sentenced to a custodial punishment. The chapter will first explore issues surrounding the prevalence of autistic individuals in prisons; then consider the challenging and supportive features of prison life for autistic individuals, as well as implications for prison-based rehabilitation.

Autism Prevalence in Prisons

Autism prevalence estimates have been found to vary across the criminal justice system (CJS) and are yet to be reliably established (Archer & Hurley, 2013; Moloney & Gulati, 2019; Robertson & McGillivray, 2015). Much of the extant prevalence research has tended to focus specifically on Asperger syndrome diagnoses in secure hospital settings. For example, studies in

2 See Introduction chapter for more on this term.

secure hospital settings and psychiatric facilities have estimated autism prevalence figures ranging between 1.4% and 18% (Enyati et al., 2008; Hare et al., 1999; Rutten et al., 2017; Scragg & Shah, 1994; Siponmaa et al., 2001; Søderstrom et al., 2004; Søndenaa et al., 2014). Despite the wide-ranging variance in estimates, there is a degree of consensus that autistic individuals are overrepresented in the broader CJS context (Cooper et al., 2022; King & Murphy, 2014; Loureiro et al., 2018; Payne et al., 2020), with figures tending to average higher than the 1%–2% prevalence often reported in the general population (Brugha et al., 2011; Centers for Disease Control and Prevention, 2020). Similarly, whilst there has been some discrepancy in reported prevalence rates (see Underwood et al., 2016) and there are meth-odological inconsistencies between studies, in the relatively small body of research that has investigated prevalence of autistic individuals serving prison sentences, the suggestion that there is overrepresentation pervades, with an estimated prevalence of up to 8.5% (Ashworth, 2016; Fazio et al., 2012; Robinson et al., 2012; Young et al., 2018).

Beyond the limited empirical research base, it has been suggested that, in practice, additional factors complicate prevalence estimations in prisons. Of these, the effective and accurate identification of autistic indi-viduals entering prisons and serving sentences has been a critical factor. Whilst there are pockets of exception, many English and Welsh prisons do not have standard routine autism screening processes in place. This is further complicated by an absence of autism screening tools empirically validated for use in prison settings (Archer & Hurley, 2013; Ashworth, 2016; Moloney & Gulati, 2019; Newman et al., 2019), resource restric-tions for more rigorous screening (Ashworth, 2016; Moloney & Gulati, 2019; Underwood et al., 2016) and difficulties acquiring developmental histories for some prisoners (Ashworth, 2016; Underwood et al., 2016, 2013). As such, there have been consistent calls in the field for augmen-tation of autism screening processes and tools in prisons (Cooper et al., 2022; Michna & Trestman, 2016; Newman et al., 2019), as well as more comprehensive approaches to autism screening and identification at the earlier stages of the criminal justice process (e.g., police custody; Criminal Justice Joint Inspection, 2021).

In addition to the absence of validated screening tools and routine screening processes, there are further factors that have contributed towards the autism identification problem in prisons. For instance, autism awareness and understanding among CJS staff (including prison staff) is often lim-ited (Ashworth, 2016; Criminal Justice Joint Inspection, 2021; McCarthy et al., 2015; Newman et al., 2019). This limited awareness and understanding can contribute towards issues such as the misattribution of autistic traits to other diagnosable mental health conditions (Allen et al., 2008), as well as other forms of misinterpretation of autistic individuals (see 'Autistic Individuals' Experiences of Prison' section later in this chapter). There are exceptions to this, with pockets of excellence to be found in some establishments (see 'Prison Autism Accreditation' section later in this chapter), and autism awareness training in development or taking place within prison services. Also, prison staff with personal experience of interacting with autistic friends or family members have been found, unsurprisingly, to exhibit greater autism awareness and understanding (Allely & Wood, 2022). Nevertheless, the implication of limited awareness and understanding is that it likely serves to compromise effective recognition of autism in prisons. This is only further complicated by how some autistic individuals may actively mask their traits as a form of adaptation to the prison context and how autistic traits (such as a preference for sameness) may be masked by a highly structured prison environment (Ashworth, 2016; Higgs & Carter, 2015).

Collectively, this complex interaction of factors likely contributes towards an underrecognition of autism in prison settings and challenges establishing prevalence figures. To compound this, the average age of autism diagnosis for autistic adults in forensic populations is 25–31 years (Helverschou et al., 2015; Murphy, 2007), which is considerably older than the mean age of diagnosis reported in non-forensic populations (3–10 years; Daniels and Mandell, 2014). Moreover, a large proportion of autistic individuals are only diagnosed once they have come into contact with the CJS (75% in Kumagami & Matsuura, 2009). Consequently, when considered in light of the autism recognition issues discussed throughout this section, it is entirely likely that there may be a hidden population of undiagnosed autistic individuals who are serving prison sentences (de la Cuesta, 2010; Myers, 2004), but are perhaps not being managed or supported appropriately (Ashworth, 2016; Mouridsen, 2012; Newman et al., 2019).

Prison Autism Accreditation

A welcomed development with regard to autism-related provisions in English and Welsh prison settings has been the introduction of the National Autistic Society (NAS) autism accreditation scheme for prisons (Hughes, 2019; Lewis et al., 2015, 2016). The NAS autism accreditation scheme was originally devised as a quality assurance programme to ensure that autistic individuals receive adequate support across a variety of organisational settings (Lewis et al., 2015; NAS, 2021). To be accredited, organisations must pass a rigorous auditing process to assess the extent of an organisation's commitment to understanding autism, supporting autistic individuals and engaging in autism-oriented practice. Organisations can be awarded one of three accreditation statuses ('aspiring,' 'accredited' or 'advanced'), and are reassessed periodically thereafter to ensure that standards and provisions are maintained. Historically, the opportunity to achieve autism accreditation was open to a variety of organisations and settings (for example, educational settings, healthcare settings and residential services). However, more recently, English and Welsh prisons have been working towards achieving autism accreditation (Hughes, 2016; Lewis et al., 2015).

The development of prison-specific NAS autism accreditation standards began in 2014 at HM Youth Offender Institute Feltham, and centred on autism-related adjustments and awareness across four key areas of the prison: education, mental health, primary care and discipline (Hughes, 2016; Lewis et al., 2015, 2016). Subsequently, the standards were successfully piloted in three more prisons (HMP Parc, HMP Wakefield and HMP Dovegate), and autism accreditation has since been pursued (and in some cases attained) in several other prison establishments (for example, HMP Whatton). Some examples of adjustments made by prisons to meet these autism accreditation standards have included the roll out of autism awareness training for staff and prisoners, low-stimulus rooms for de-escalation and 'timeout' opportunities for autistic prisoners, and permitting autistic prisoners with sensory sensitivities to noise to wear ear defenders (Hughes, 2019; Lewis et al., 2016). These changes could be regarded as those adjustments to context endorsed by the social model view of autism (discussed earlier in this chapter), and thereby represent a shift away from a medical model focus on changing the individual to suit a prison. With regard to the benefits and consequences of these changes; though yet to be published, it is anticipated that the implementation of these standards and adjustments will undergo a formal evaluation, across a variety of outcome measures, including

> use of force, in levels of violence, adjudications and negative reports; safety for prisoners with autism, other prisoners and staff; barriers to engagement with prisoners with autism; effects on rehabilitation, early release and rates of re-offending; management of co-morbid health issues for prisoners with autism; and staff sickness rates.
>
> (Lewis et al., 2016, p. 77)

Although the NAS autism accreditation scheme has been a promising development and is receiving increasing attention from prisons, there is limited evidence of analogous schemes operating in prisons outside of England and Wales. Although not necessarily enshrined in an official accreditation or certification programme, there is nevertheless evidence from other jurisdictions that recognises the unique support and management needs of autistic prisoners (for example, in Norway; Helverschou et al., 2018). As such, the identification and comparison of good practice between different international jurisdictions may constitute a useful area for future research and may offer an opportunity for cross-jurisdictional learning. Furthermore, whilst there are evident examples of good practice in those prisons that have achieved (or are actively pursuing) NAS autism accreditation, this does not detract from the importance of recognising challenges faced by, and supporting the needs of, autistic prisoners more generally. As such, these challenges and support needs are a key focus of the remainder of this chapter.

Autistic Individuals' Experiences of Prison

Historically, there has been a scarcity of research relating to understanding the experiences and needs of autistic individuals serving prison sentences. However, in recent years, with increased research interest in supporting autistic individuals in the CJS more broadly (for example, Crane et al., 2016; George et al., 2018; Gibbs & Haas, 2020; Salerno & Schuller, 2019), there has been a similar increased interest in the experiences and needs of autistic individuals in prisons (for example, Allely & Wood, 2022; Helverschou et al., 2018; Newman et al., 2015, 2019; Vinter, 2020; Vinter et al., 2020). Collectively, research has suggested that autistic individuals who come into contact with the CJS (including prisons) may face additional challenges, have diverse management needs, and may require additional support through the criminal justice process. This section of the chapter explores and discusses the elements of the autistic prison experience that can be challenging and/or supportive, and is largely derived from research that has focused on the lived experiences of autistic individuals serving prison sentences. This will focus on three core aspects of life in custody: communication and social interactions; routines, rules and predictability; and sensory environment.

Communication and Social Interactions

One element of the prison experience that has been found to present challenges for autistic prisoners is navigating the complex social environment. Specifically, research exploring the lived experiences of autistic prisoners has found that they can often encounter challenges during interpersonal interactions with both other prisoners and prison staff (Helverschou et al., 2018; Newman et al., 2015; Vinter et al., 2020). Autistic prisoners often report experiences of encountering misunderstandings or altercations with others in the prison, often believing that this is because they struggle to 'read' others' intentions and feelings, or are unsure how to respond appropriately (Vinter, 2020; Vinter et al., 2020; Michna & Trestman, 2016). For example, autistic prisoners have referred to inadvertently causing offence to prison staff or other prisoners, because they are perceived to be too blunt or direct in their responses to questions, which in turn can be interpreted as disrespectful. This type of situation can escalate into altercations where tensions rise and others become confrontational, but autistic prisoners report finding it difficult to recognise or accurately interpret implicit social cues that otherwise indicate said escalation (for example, body language or tone of voice) until it is too late.

These challenges are further exacerbated by the complex, sometimes volatile, nature of a prison social environment, which may be rife with deception, humour, implicit communication, and other nuanced or unpredictable types of communication, which autistic individuals may struggle to discern. For example, an autistic prisoner may find it difficult to distinguish jokes from more serious communication or may find it tricky to discern whether someone is being deceptive (Vinter, 2020). As a consequence of these various social demands, autistic prisoners can experience difficulties establishing and maintaining positive relations with others in the prison. Autistic prisoners have reported negative experiences of feeling and being treated differently to others in the prison (particularly their neurotypical counterparts), sometimes resulting in associated experiences of alienation, social isolation and bullying (Allely, 2015; Newman et al., 2019; Talbot, 2009). Furthermore, it has been suggested that some autistic prisoners can find it difficult to report or communicate these negative experiences to staff when they are in need of support (Lewis et al., 2015). As a result, autistic prisoners may isolate themselves, purposefully avoid social interactions with others or may otherwise simply lack confidence to engage in social interactions with others (Allely & Wood, 2022; Helverschou et al., 2018; Newman et al., 2015). Although many of these issues can and do exist for autistic individuals in various other social contexts, the uniquely complex, and sometimes dangerous, prison social environment can have much more impactful ramifications for autistic individuals living in prisons compared to other contexts (e.g., a heightened sense of threat to personal safety). On the other hand, it should be noted that challenges associated with the social environment are not ubiquitously experienced in the same way by all autistic prisoners. Some autistic individuals have reported positive experiences of a prison social environment; for example, several autistic prisoners in studies by Vinter (2020) and Vinter et al. (2020) believed that they had become more socially active since arriving in prison compared to their lives outside of prison. A critical factor in these positive social experiences was a sense of understanding, acceptance and supportiveness conveyed by other prisoners and prison staff. Being surrounded by others in the prison who were supportive of autism creates an enabling context for some autistic prisoners to become more socially confident and active, thereby mitigating some of the aforementioned negative impacts of being autistic in the prison environment.

This takes us onto the final point to be addressed in this section of the chapter, namely, the appropriate perspective for regarding these issues. When considered through a purely diagnostic, medicalised view, challenges for autistic individuals in negotiating the social realm of a prison make intuitive sense; after all, from this perspective, autism is a condition characterised by 'persistent deficits in social communication and social interaction' (APA, 2013, p. 50). As such, it is tempting to attribute these challenges to a core 'impairment' possessed by autistic prisoners. However, when considered through the alternative social model view described in the introduction to this chapter, the picture becomes more complex. Whilst an autistic individuals' difficulties in reading others seem to be relevant to the challenges they face in the prison social arena, the social context itself is also relevant. Difficulties seem to stem not just from how an autistic individual interacts with the social environment, but how others in the social environment reciprocate during interpersonal interactions. A pattern in what seems to underpin autistic prisoners' negative experiences of social interactions with prison staff and other prisoners has been a lack of understanding shown by others (Vinter, 2020; Vinter et al., 2020).

These issues resonate with the 'double empathy problem' concept (discussed in Chapter 1; Mitchel et al., 2021), which emphasises that difficulties in social interactions are reciprocal and are as much about neurotypical others not understanding an autistic individual, as they are about an autistic individual finding it difficult to understand others. Autistic prisoners report experiences of feeling misunderstood by others in the prison, or others showing an apparent reluctance to try to understand their perspective or accommodate their autism, relying instead on making assumptions. For example, during an interaction, an autistic individual's behaviour may be interpreted at face value by prison staff as wilful defiance, argumentativeness and rigidity, and may then reprimand them accordingly. However, in some cases, these outward behaviours may in fact reflect underlying anxieties about a stress-inducing situation the autistic individual feels they are in. Their 'rigidity' may therefore be an expression of this internal experience, where they perhaps otherwise struggle to explicitly verbalise these feelings. By contrast, positive experiences of the prison social environment are often characterised by interactions where others convey a clear willingness to listen to and understand an autistic prisoner's perspective, making efforts to adapt communication and/or facilitate an autistic individual's communication. These issues are also indicative of the importance of considering the impact of broader autism awareness in prisons, and the potential value of increasing autism awareness amongst prison staff and prisoners to enhance the social climate experience for autistic individuals. In summary, the social aspect of prison life forms an important dimension of autistic prisoners' experiences of prison. Whilst prima facie, it could be speculated that this social aspect is inherently fraught with challenges for autistic prisoners, evidence suggests that factors such as autism understanding and acceptance from others can be critically influential factors in the quality of these experiences. In the extreme negative, a less supportive social atmosphere that is characterised by an unwillingness to understanding or accommodate neurodivergence may be more conducive to the emergence of challenges for autistic prisoners. By contrast, a prison social atmosphere characterised by autism understanding and acceptance can be a supportive feature of the prison experience for autistic prisoners, enabling them to become more socially confident and active. In accordance with the social model view, this has emphasised the importance of considering context when seeking to understand the challenges experienced by autistic individuals in prisons, rather than solely attributing challenges to 'deficits' within an individual (i.e., the medical model perspective).

Routines, Rules and Predictability

Another facet of the prison experience that has been found to be critical for many autistic prisoners is the routines and rules that govern prison life (Allely, 2015; Allely & Wood, 2022; McAdam, 2012; Newman et al., 2015; Vinter et al., 2020). The presence of routine and structures in everyday life is commonly considered to be helpful for autistic individuals. An established routine can be helpful for autistic individuals to experience a sense of predictability and sameness, in an otherwise less-than-predictable social world. In a similar vein, prison environments are typically highly structured and routine based, and therefore could be presumed to be a supportive context for autistic individuals serving prison sentences. However, whilst this is true to some degree, evidence suggests that the rules and routines that govern prison life can sometimes also be a source of challenge for autistic prisoners.

Prison life is, by and large, governed by an imposed structured daily routine. This routine is comprised of designated times for aspects of prison life, such as meal times; unlocking and locking cells; recreation time; and purposeful activity such as work, education and movement around the prison. Whilst there is naturally some variation between different prison sites, at a local level, within a single prison site, the routine is typically advertised as a fixed timetable. For example, unlock time (that is, the time when prisoners' cell doors are unlocked and they are permitted to be out of their cells) may be designated as 8 am. At an individual level, a prisoner may then go to work or education activities, before returning around noon for lunch, and so on. This rigidly timetabled lifestyle has been experienced by some autistic prisoners as a supportive feature of the prison environment, adding a comforting sense of consistency and sameness, helping an autistic prisoner to know what to expect and what is expected of them (Helverschou et al., 2018). Conversely, however, the prison routine can be regarded as a source of challenge for autistic prisoners (Allely & Wood, 2022; Vinter, 2020; Vinter et al., 2020). Challenges tend to arise where there is a disconnect between the routine as advertised and how the routine may operate in reality. Whilst the routine is advertised as rigidly adhered to, it is nevertheless prone to sudden disruption and delay at broader and individual levels (Allely & Wood, 2022; Cashin & Newman, 2009; Newman et al., 2015; Vinter et al., 2020). For example, there may be unanticipated delays in cell unlock times in the mornings or the entire prison may go on a sudden lockdown for security reasons. At an individual level, a prisoner may experience situations like short notice cancellations of appointments or relatively sudden announcements of cell arrangement changes (for example, new cell mates or moving cells). Moreover, in transitioning from their life in the community after being sentenced, an autistic prisoner may struggle to adapt to the prison routine in the first place. As a punishment designed to reduce liberty, it is inevitable that the move from life outside of prison to life inside is characterised by a lot of change, which can be difficult for any prisoner. For an autistic individual who depends on a sense of sameness and predictability in their daily routine, this transition can come with additional challenges; particularly if the new prison routine does not align well with personal routines they have adhered to in life on the outside. Research exploring the prison experiences of autistic prisoners has consistently found that these various sources of disruption, inconsistency and change can be experienced as challenging by autistic prisoners, resulting in feelings of distress, anxiety and frustration. To cope with the sense of unpredictability associated with the broader prison routine, and to reinstall a sense of stability or sameness, some autistic prisoners attempt to develop self-imposed routines or contingency plans that can operate within the broader fluctuating prison routines, to varying degrees of success (Newman et al., 2015; Vinter, 2020; Vinter et al., 2020).

The challenges associated with disruption, inconsistency and change in the prison routine are often compounded by what is perceived as a lack of corresponding information or explanation. That is, autistic prisoners frequently report the absence of sufficient information to prepare them for, or help them to make sense of, changes to the prison routine. Anecdotally, these issues extend to the prison reception process, whereby it is not always made clear what is happening or what is going to happen at each stage of the process. Autistic prisoners have described this experience as particularly anxiety inducing, as they may be asked to sit in holding cells for prolonged periods, or be asked to attend different rooms or desks, sometimes overwhelmed with the number of questions they are asked, with little explanation offered about the process in return. Ultimately, autistic prisoners place value on having access to clearly communicated advance notice of what to expect and what will be expected of them in most aspects of prison life. Specifically, in this context, autistic prisoners appreciate advance warning that a change in routine is going to happen before it does or some degree of explanation of why a sudden change has occurred (Allely & Wood, 2022; Vinter, 2020). From the prison staff perspective, this may not always be feasible (e.g., in the event of a sudden prison lockdown due to a live security threat). However, at the very least, being told what to expect next can be a valuable measure to help autistic prisoners to cope with a sudden change. Furthermore, during processes like the reception process, autistic prisoners appreciate the opportunity to be given concrete indications of what the process will involve, how long each step should take and the opportunity to ask questions.

Rules are another related facet of the prison experience that can be challenging for autistic prisoners. Again, much like the issues described earlier, these challenges revolve around issues of communication and consistency. Specifically, whilst prison rules seem, prima facie, to offer structure and predictability to prison life, they can be a source of difficulty for autistic prisoners if they are vaguely conveyed, interpreted overly literally or inconsistently applied (Newman et al., 2015). For example, in many prisons, prisoners will have access to a cell bell to gain the attention of officers on the wing. Often this bell will be advertised as for emergencies only, however, what constitutes an emergency may be left broad and unspecified, or may be interpreted and applied inconsistently among different officers. This can result in autistic prisoners experiencing uncertainty in whether or not to use the bell, even where its use is warranted; equally, it can lead to challenging interactions with officers if they are deemed to have used the bell inappropriately, albeit inadvertently. This is just one example of many of how limited concrete guidance around rules and inconsistent application of rules can be difficult for autistic prisoners to adjust to and adhere to during their daily life in prison.

Finally, prison rules can serve to restrict the pursuit of highly focused interests. For example, materials needed for an individual to pursue an interest in model vehicles may be largely prohibited in cells for security reasons. Whilst this makes sense from a security perspective, it can nevertheless be problematic where those interests can offer an avenue of self-soothing comfort or coping with other challenging aspects of the prison experience. This can be further exacerbated where an explanation is perhaps not clearly offered to the individual as to why an interest cannot be pursued. In situations where this is a challenge for autistic prisoners, it has been recognised that alternative avenues to pursue interests may be a viable support measure. It may be that pursuit of interests could be facilitated through thoughtful job allocation, activity groups or workshops that relate to the interest, or an alternative means of pursuing interests in the cell (for example, building model vehicles replaced with provision of books about model vehicles), tailored according to the individual.

In summary, whilst the preceding discussion may largely convey an impression that prison routines and rules as intrinsically associated with challenges for autistic prisoners, it is important to emphasise that they can be supportive features too. Quality of communication can be a crucial factor in determining whether these features are experienced as challenging or supportive. Many of the issues highlighted centre on the critical importance of knowing what to expect and knowing what is expected of them, with clarity, concreteness and consistency of communication being integral to achieving this. In alignment with the social model perspective, the impact of prison routines and rules outlined in this section has further illustrated the role of context in determining whether and how autistic individuals can experience challenges in prisons, as well as how adjustments to that context may be beneficial for many autistic prisoners.

Sensory Environment

The final aspect of the prison context that has been found to be impactful for autistic prisoners is the sensory environment (Allely & Wood, 2022; Robertson & McGillivray, 2015; Vinter, 2020; Vinter et al., 2020). Sensory differences, manifesting as sensory hypersensitivity (that is, heightened reactivity) and hyposensitivity (that is, lower reactivity), are common, albeit diverse, in autistic individuals and can have challenging implications for autistic prisoners living in a prison setting. These sensory issues can span a variety of sensory inputs, including light, sound, touch and smell, but there are some specific inputs that will be discussed in this section which have been found to be particularly problematic in prison settings. Of these, hypersensitivity to the inescapable and excessive noise in custody has been regarded as one of the most impactful sensory experiences for autistic prisoners (Allely & Wood, 2022; Vinter, 2020; Vinter et al., 2020). This includes aversive experiences stemming from both specific noises in the auditory environment (such as others whistling, alarms, the sound of a cell door unlocking and jangling keys) and more general noise in the prison (such as overlapping voices, shouting and clanking gates in busy wing areas). Autistic prisoners frequently express a wish to be able to retreat from the noise or obtain a means of blocking it out, often resigning themselves to its inescapability. These experiences have been associated with feelings of distress, anxiety, frustration and even negative somatic experiences (such as nausea). Whilst non-autistic prisoners may find that they adjust and acclimatise to the noises over time, autistic prisoners may not be able to habituate themselves so easily (Allely & Wood, 2022). Other aspects of the prison sensory environment that have been regarded as challenging for autistic prisoners, and may serve to distress or impact adjustment to prison life, have included increased sensitivity to light (such as fluorescent lighting), smell (such as perfumes, body sprays, air fresheners and cleaning products) and touch (such as prison clothing, bedding textures and physical restraint by staff).

Beyond the internal difficulties that autistic prisoners may experience on a personal level in response to the prison environment, there are also further implications that may lead to additional challenging experiences, namely, how an autistic prisoner's reaction to aversive sensory experiences are interpreted by others in the prison. When an autistic prisoner is, for example, feeling overwhelmed by a distressing auditory experience, it may not be immediately clear to others who do not experience sensory difficulties in the same way (for example, prison staff), particularly if the individual does not verbalise this. Consequently, they may naturally make assumptions and attribute motivations based on surface-level behaviours. This can be understood using the iceberg analogy (see Figure 4.3) often used in TEACCH-based approaches (Treatment and Education of Autistic and related Communication-handicapped Children; Mesibov et al., 2005). In this analogy, the section of the iceberg above the waterline represents the observable behaviours of an autistic prisoner, and the larger section below the waterline represents that prisoner's internal experiences and underlying reasons for that behaviour.

Using this analogy, during an interaction, a prison officer may see an autistic prisoner seeming not to listen or actively covering their ears (represented by the iceberg above the water's surface), and may interpret these behaviours as representing wilful ignorance, disrespect, acting out or non-compliance. In doing so, the officer may not recognise that below the water's surface, an autistic prisoner is having a distressing sensory experience and is simply attempting to block out the problematic noise. As a result, by relying on their initial surface-level interpretation, without malicious intent, they may reprimand the autistic prisoner for their apparent non-compliance. This further emphasises the critical role of both awareness and communication

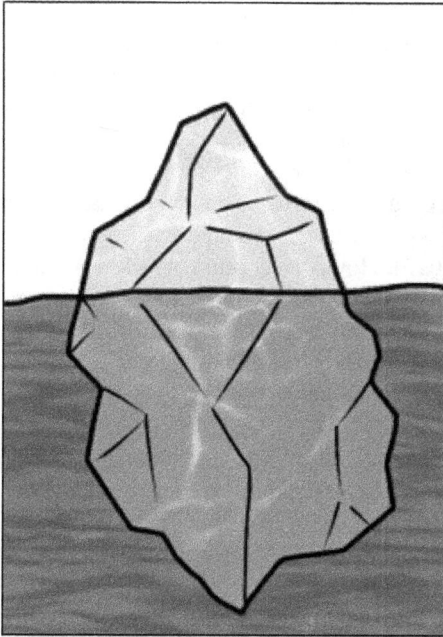

Figure 4.3 Visualisation of the iceberg analogy (Vinter, 2020, p. 248).

in managing an autistic prisoner's experience of prison, and the importance of recognising the two-way nature of communication. In this example, challenges arise not just from how an autistic individual communicates their distressing internal experience, but also how others around that individual receive and respond to that communication. Autistic prisoners have described other problematic ways that others in the prison have interpreted or treated them differently due to their sensory-related behaviours (Vinter, 2020). Examples include other prisoners mocking or excessively questioning autistic prisoners if they choose to wear tinted eyeglasses as a means of coping with hypersensitivity to artificial lighting. These experiences have led to autistic prisoners reporting feelings of alienation, humiliation or otherwise unable to utilise means of coping with sensory difficulties for fear of mockery or othering.

In summary, reports of autistic prisoners encountering aversive sensory experiences in the prison context highlight the importance of recognition of and accommodation or adjustment by the prison estate and its staff to these needs. Evidently, this is not only of importance for mitigating the immediate distressing impact for an autistic prisoner on an internal level, but is also important to avoid secondary challenges during interactions with others in the prison, which could ultimately compromise the well-being of prisoners, staff and the fundamental purposes of custody (such as rehabilitation). Accommodation and adjustment to support individuals with sensory differences can take a variety of forms. In a more literal, tangible sense, the provision of things like ear defenders, quiet movement periods, avoidance of perfumes or fragrances, greater reliance on natural lighting (or provision of LED lighting), or low-stimulus areas could be beneficial for some autistic prisoners (Vinter, 2020). However, it must be acknowledged that these may not always be feasible, depending on resource or security restrictions. On the other hand, accommodation of sensory differences could also take the form of broader education, training and increased awareness in the prison for both staff and other prisoners. That is, fostering a social climate of acceptance and understanding of differences could be beneficial to autistic prisoners (and other neurodivergent prisoners). This could encourage others to avoid making erroneous assumptions, to consider alternative explanations for surface-level behaviours (see Figure 4.3), and/or could help autistic prisoners to feel greater self-acceptance and comfortability when employing strategies to cope with aversive sensory experiences. Though it is conceded that this may be a challenging strategy to execute in some prisons, where the social climate is perhaps particularly complex, volatile or otherwise resistant to change. Finally, sensory issues do not always have to be about challenges. Whilst sensory avoidance can be an impactful aspect of the prison experience for some autistic prisoners, equally, sensory-seeking could be utilised as a force of good. Specifically, an individual may have sensory inputs (or sensations) that they actively seek out and take comfort in (for example, a tactile preference for the feeling of a specific fabric texture). Facilitating sensory-seeking could be a supportive measure to help autistic prisoners to cope with more challenging experiences during their sentence (such as providing a square of that fabric for self-soothing purposes), subject to security and resource restrictions. However, as sensory-seeking and self-soothing behaviours can also be subject to stigma and exploitation from others (Kapp et al., 2019), such accommodations would likely benefit from concurrent measures to enhance autism awareness and encourage acceptance in the prisons more broadly.

Implications for Prison-Based Rehabilitation

Despite the growing literature base pertaining to autistic individuals' experiences of prison, limited empirical research has explored issues and nuances surrounding prison-based rehabilitation for autistic prisoners.

However, recent empirical evidence from Vinter (2020) has highlighted how the challenging and supportive aspects of the prison experience discussed throughout this chapter can have important implications for how and whether autistic prisoners engage with rehabilitative interventions. This evidence suggests that prison-based rehabilitation does not occur in a vacuum. That is, the quality of interventions, experiences and outcomes are not solely determined by what happens in the confines of the offending behaviour programme (OBP) itself. Elements of the prison context can be impactful (both positively and negatively) upon an autistic prisoner's readiness for and engagement with interventions. Therefore, the impact of the broader prison experience of autistic prisoners should be considered.

Specifically, Vinter's (2020) findings suggested that social interactions with prison staff and other prisoners, consistency in the daily routine and regime, the prison physical and sensory environment, autism awareness, and availability of support provisions played important roles in mediating mental well-being for autistic prisoners (particularly anxiety and mood). It was further suggested that poorer mental well-being could impact how and whether autistic prisoners engaged with interventions to address offending. For example, an autistic prisoner's experiences of a troubling social interaction on the wing or disrupted routine on the morning prior to an OBP session could have a ripple effect on how, or indeed whether, they engaged with that session. Evidence from Vinter (2020) suggested that autistic prisoners can dwell upon the negative thoughts and feelings associated with these experiences and bring them into the session with them. Autistic prisoners who experienced more anxiety, stemming from the broader prison experience, seemed to be less willing to participate in OBPs, felt overwhelmed and/or disengaged, or became disruptive during OBPs. Therefore, it could be inferred from these findings that the broader prison experience can have a countertherapeutic effect for autistic prison-ers, reducing any benefit they may have been otherwise able to reap from such interventions. By contrast, autistic prisoners who felt well-supported by a cohesive network of prison staff and other prisoners seemed to have more positive prison-based intervention experiences. In particular, these networks of support were characterised by relations with others who con-veyed a sense of understanding and acceptance of who they were, what they found challenging and what their strengths were. This example illus-trates how, under the right circumstances, the prison context is also capable of being conducive to engagement in rehabilitation for autistic prisoners. Vinter (2020) conceptualised this as, potentially, an example of an interac-tion between internal and external treatment readiness conditions, under Ward et al.'s (2004) multifactor offender readiness model (MORM; see Figure 4.4).

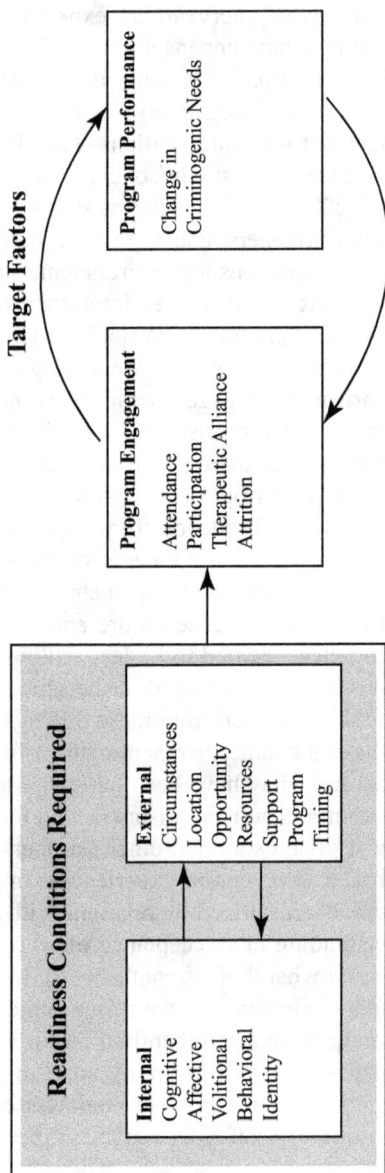

Figure 4.4 Multifactor offender readiness model (MORM) (Ward et al., 2004, p. 650).

In summary, it is clear that the broader prison context can be a critical consideration when working with autistic individuals in prison-based interventions to address offending. However, whilst evidence indicates that the prison experience can be impactful on an autistic prisoner's rehabilitation, the delivery of an intervention is a similarly important consideration (Vinter, 2020). For example, group-based OBPs were found to be a common challenge for autistic prisoners, often contributing towards autistic prisoners feeling overwhelmed, a finding which resonated with existing literature from beyond the prison context (Higgs & Carter, 2015; Milton et al., 2002; Radley & Shaherbano, 2011). Similarly, content that centred on emotions and feelings was also regarded as challenging for autistic prisoners, particularly where it relied heavily on verbal delivery methods, and therefore required adapted delivery styles (for example, the use of visual delivery methods and more concrete examples grounded in autistic individuals' experiences or interests). Additionally, there are other elements of OBP delivery that relate to the broader prison context but are not exclusive to the prison context, such as challenges posed by the sensory environment in OBP sessions and the availability of information about OBPs for prisoners prior to commencement. Crucially, however, it was the synergy between the broader prison experience and OBP delivery that was vital for autistic prisoners to flourish in interventions, and, by contrast, it was discord within (or between) these two that could compromise the quality of interventions experiences for autistic prisoners.

Conclusions and Recommendations

This chapter has explored some of the key issues and implications relevant to autism in prisons. It discussed broader issues relating to the prevalence and identification of autistic individuals in prisons, the NAS autism accreditation scheme, and the specific challenging and supportive features of prison life for autistic individuals, as well as implications for prison-based rehabilitation. From this, themes that emerged centred on the importance of autism awareness and understanding from others, the crucial underpinning role that communication can play in many of the challenges experienced by autistic prisoners, and the need for supportive adjustments or accommodations in the prison context for autistic prisoners. Enhancing autism training and awareness in prisons is arguably one of the most fundamental priorities in relation to autism in prisons. Several of the issues raised in this chapter can be traced back to the presence or absence of good autism awareness, and acceptance and understanding from prison staff and other prisoners. Consequently, in recent years, key recommendations for practice in the CJS (including prisons) have consistently centred on increased autism awareness training and education (McCarthy et al., 2015; Michna & Trestman, 2016; Robertson & McGillivray, 2015; Underwood et al., 2016; Vinter et al., 2020). It is the contention of this chapter that this should remain a priority in prisons and that training should be informed by the voices of, and designed in collaboration with, autistic prisoners to ensure that it is resonant with their needs and experiences.

Furthermore, many of the challenging prison experiences for autistic prisoners, and those staff working with them, seem to be underpinned by issues relating to communication. This includes issues where an autistic prisoner may struggle to understand the communication of others in the prison, or may not have their own attempts at communication understood, whether that be during interpersonal social interactions or during episodes of distress (for example, during an aversive sensory experience). In another sense, this also relates to communication issues surrounding how, and whether, an autistic prisoner is kept informed about rules, routines and regimes in the prison. As such, addressing communication can also be seen as a potential route to overcoming or mitigating challenges. In a broader sense, this could take the form of people around autistic prisoners (staff and peers) making conscious efforts to avoid quick assumptions about what underpins behaviours that they regard as challenging and to consider alternative interpretations of what said behaviours could be communicating. In a more specific sense, considerations should be given to what adjustments could be made to improve how others communicate with autistic prisoners or to facilitate autistic prisoners' own communication, for example, avoiding ambiguous, non-literal language, and keeping to more concrete, direct and explicit approaches to communication. As another example, prison staff could simply offer autistic prisoners time to process information presented to them in a variety of modalities (avoiding an overreliance on verbal instruction), and being willing to take the time to enable and actively listen to responses. These principles and approaches could be embedded into autism awareness training and education.

Finally, creating a supportive and enabling context through the provision of adjustments and accommodations in the prison environment has the potential to be hugely beneficial for autistic prisoners. As just discussed, some of these include adjustments relevant to communication, such as clear communication around what to expect and what is expected of them (for example, visual timetables and timely notifications of routine changes). Other examples of accommodations include adjustments to the physical environment (such as the reduction of, or protection from, aversive sensory stimuli), and considering allocation of prison jobs that offer a suitable workplace (for example, quieter or less busy) and map onto an autistic prisoner's strengths (Vinter et al., 2020). Crucially, whilst there are prison-wide adjustments that could be made to benefit many prisoners, due to the heterogenous nature of autistic individuals, several accommodations may need to be tailored to individual needs.

Finally, whilst the issues covered in this chapter represent common themes in the literature, it is important to highlight that they are not representative of all prisons or all autistic prisoners' experiences. Autistic individuals and prison establishments alike are incredibly diverse, and there is no one-size-fits-all approach to understanding these issues or formulating recommendations. In addition, there is still work that needs to be done to understand how different types of autistic individuals experience prison and how differences in prison establishments can be relevant to how prisons are experienced by autistic prisoners. For instance, mirroring a pattern in autism and forensic research fields more generally, there is a relative absence of literature exploring female autistic prisoner experiences. Moreover, there is a need for complementary research exploring the prison experiences of other neurodivergent prisoner groups in order to understand how neurodivergent individuals experience prisons, what their support needs may be and how to address them.

To conclude, this chapter should be regarded as a preliminary insight into some of the issues that pertain to autism in prisons, the needs of autistic prisoners and recommendations for how to address those needs. It is not intended to serve as an all-encompassing or exhaustive guide, and the issues outlined may be more or less relevant depending on the autistic prisoner and the context in which they are situated. Therefore, it is crucial that prisons work collaboratively with autistic prisoners as individuals to enable them to flourish in the prison context. Moreover, when considering how best to work with and support autistic prisoners, it is important to recognise the value of paying close attention to the voices and lived experiences of autistic prisoners and the staff that work closely with them (that is, the prison autism community). The insights and recommendations conveyed in this chapter were predominantly drawn directly from the reported lived experiences of members of the prison autism community. In a similar vein, it is argued here that changes to practice and future research should be co-created with members of the prison autism community, informed by their collective voice to empower those individuals, and ensure that work is well-attuned to the needs and lived realities of members of those communities.

Conclusion

Tom Smith

Summary

Chapter 1, by Shirley Reveley and Iain Dickie, focused on 'street' policing and the implications of current practice for autistic suspects. The authors emphasise that police contact is generally stressful; this is particularly so for autistic individuals, and likely to be exacerbated in challenging situations of urgency, such as arrest or crisis. However, they note that, at present, there has been limited research on the dynamics of relationships between beat officers and autistic suspects. That which does exist suggests that officers have limited general awareness of autism, though there is some evidence of knowledge and awareness penetrating practice—but nothing to suggest this is widespread. The authors argue that officer awareness and understanding is key to both the identification of autistic individuals, who may be vulnerable, and the quality of any subsequent interactions. Identification is clearly an important first step, but appears to be hampered by various factors, including fear of disclosure, issues of 'context blindness,' and the aforementioned deficits in officers knowledge and awareness. However, the authors assert that officer perception (that is, 'the way in which professionals observe and understand the behaviour and communication of autistic people') is also important. Different perceptual frameworks of officers and autistic individuals affect interactions—this creates a gap in perceptual understanding (described as an 'empathy divide'). Research suggests limited training on autism is currently given to officers, and is neither systematic or targeted (or necessarily effective). The authors argue that an omission in that which is provided appears to be training on perceptual differences, as well as empathy and empathetic communication (an emerging area in the US). Evidence suggests such training not only builds trust and confidence, but leads to more effective interactions and outcomes. However, this needs to take account of perceptual differences (for example, the 'double empathy problem' described in the chapter). The authors suggest that training on

DOI: 10.4324/9781003248774-6

perception and empathy could overcome the aforementioned gap and allow more effective communication, with a proposed method of doing so being the use of encounter groups, that is, 'unstructured opportunity for individuals to meet and hear the thoughts, feelings, and perspectives of others within the group.' The chapter concludes by underlining that more research is needed on both officer training as well as street-level police/autistic interactions, and that any training should involve lived experience input.

Chapter 2, by Clare Allely and David Murphy, focuses on the interviewing of autistic suspects in police custody. Research generally suggests that autistic individuals come into contact with the criminal justice system (CJS) at a higher rate and that autistic suspects are particularly vulnerable in an interrogation context. If police officers do not recognise and adapt to the vulnerability of autistic individuals in custody or during interviews, the suspect is likely to experience distress and there is likely to be a negative impact on the forensic process of interview. As such, the authors argue that aspects of autism can lead to barriers to engagement and misinterpretations by officers, potentially leading to negative (and incorrect) resolutions to investigations. Common characteristics of autism reviewed in the chapter include impairment of understanding, issues with sequential memory and recall, communication differences, the impact of sensory overload, challenges in being able to comply, unusual emotional and verbal expression, issues with time pressure, and repetitive behaviours and restricted interests (RBRIs). If an autistic suspect presents these characteristics in interview, this can lead officers to conclude the suspect is evasive, lying, guilty, suspicious or delinquent; alternatively, an overly compliant suspect may be vulnerable to making false admissions of guilt. The authors conclude the chapter by suggesting a number of issues that investigative interviewers should consider when interviewing autistic suspects to enhance fairness and quality and lower distress. For example, it is suggested the personal safety of participants can be enhanced by engaging with family and other relevant figures of the suspect to understand the suspect more fully. It is argued that interviews should be broken up into multiple, shorter parts and should be scheduled carefully to fit the suspect's routines. Officers should also engage with the suspect and others to manage any sensory issues, including by adapting the physical environment, considering times of day that are quieter in custody for interviews, considering limiting the use of physical contact; moderating the tone and volume of voice, and allowing suspects to use sensory aids and engage in stimming. The authors acknowledge that autistic individuals vary widely in presentation, but suggest that some basic approaches can be adopted and then built upon to tailor to the particular suspect. It is argued that effective communication requires officers to have advance knowledge about the suspect. Relevant adaptations might include use of intermediaries, nonverbal communication methods, careful choice of language, ensuring the purpose and rules of interview are clear; providing time for processing and response, and carefully considering question style. The authors conclude by asserting that these potential challenges highlight the importance of well-trained interviewers, but suggest that this is currently a deficit in provision.

Chapter 3, by Clare Allely, Eddie Chaplin, Jody Salter, Jane McCarthy and Felicity Gerry, examines autistic defendants in the context of criminal courts. As both a recognised disability and form of neurodivergence, autism can leave defendants significantly vulnerable and disadvantaged in the context of the CJS. The authors suggest that criminal courts are not autism-friendly, with the result being that they are experienced negatively by autistic defendants and that there is a risk that their fair-trial rights may be undermined. The chapter challenges the pervasive oversimplification of autism by reference to types of 'functioning,' an approach which can lead to both failure to recognise vulnerability and barriers to fair trials. Instead, the authors suggest that more focus needs to be placed on variable profiles with strengths and weaknesses, with a more tailored and nuanced approach adopted. The chapter emphasises that fair trials are fundamental but can be affected by autistic presentation, failure to ensure adaptation of processes, and the impact of being autistic on legal and factual issues at trial. First, the chapter highlights that identification of autistic defendants can be an issue due to autism being heterogenous, lack of knowledge and training on the part of CJS professionals, and a lack of detailed information about the defendant being provided to courts. Whilst information about a defendant may be lacking—and thus hamper adaptation of trials—provision of information can also confuse and undermine fairness, for example, if extensive, medicalised detail about autism is provided to juries. There is currently a lack of understanding about how bias affects decision-making in this context. During trial, autistic presentation (behaviour, communication, expression, processing time, memory) may be misinterpreted or negatively perceived by judges and jurors, leading to unfair and inaccurate outcomes. As such, taking no action to address this can undermine a fair trial. The authors argue that courts should be willing to use their inherent jurisdiction to use special measures to address this and that defence advocates need to actively engage in protecting their autistic clients' fair-trial rights.

In terms of the nature of alleged offending, particular areas of concern highlighted in the chapter are radicalised offending and complicity crime, with culpability of autistic defendants accused of such crimes needing to be carefully considered. To demonstrate, the chapter examines the case studies of *Dunleavy* and *Henry*. It is argued that detailed exploration of the interplay between autistic traits and alleged offending is vital to fair and accurate decisions, and that the role of experts is crucial here, a notable deficit in both cases. Finally, the role of Liaison and Diversion (L&D) services is considered, with the authors highlighting that there currently appears to be significant variation in provision and approach, which is hindered by a lack of screening for autism across the CJS and limited assessment capacity and expertise. It is argued that effective screening would allow identification of vulnerability, preparation of reports for courts and appropriate adaptations to be made. These can also affect material issues of evidence (such as in the case studies). As such, L&D services need to consider how they engage with autistic individuals, including managing any comorbidities, underlining that there is a need for specialist staff to be embedded within L&D services.

Chapter 4, by Luke P Vinter and Gayle Dillon, considers, through a social model lens, the challenges faced by autistic individuals in prison settings. In contrast, a medical model has previously pervaded approaches to autistic individuals, focusing on deficits intrinsically linked to autism. Instead, the social model recognises the differences in autistic individuals and that barriers/challenges are intrinsically linked to context. As such, the authors argue that support and management is better directed towards context, with the focus in this chapter being on custody. The chapter opens by discussing prevalence, which it acknowledges is hard to establish. However, there is a general consensus that autistic individuals are overrepresented in the CJS, which is particularly problematic in prisons due to lack of routine screening and lack of awareness amongst prison staff (with exceptional pockets of excellence). The authors also highlight that prison environments may also mask autistic traits, as they are highly structured. To summarise, there is likely a hidden population of autistic prisoners who are not recognised, managed or supported appropriately. Attempts to address the latter have included autism accreditation, a form of quality assurance designed to improve support for autistic individuals in institutions like prisons. Adjustments designed to attain accreditation (and thereby improve experiences) have included more training for staff on autism, the provision of low-stimulus rooms, timeouts for prisoners and other sensory accommodations. The authors outline the emerging body of research on experiences of autistic prisoners, which collectively suggests they face additional challenges, have diverse management needs and may require additional support through the criminal justice process.

These primarily relate to three core aspects of life in custody: communication and social interactions; routines, rules and predictability; and sensory environment. Communication challenges can include misinterpretation by and of autistic prisoners, altercations with other prisoners, the volatile social environment of prison, being treated differently and therefore feeling isolated, and finding it difficult to report issues.

However, some research suggests that some autistic prisoners have felt empowered and understood for the first time in the prison environment. Prisons can be both highly structured and routinised, which may be helpful for autistic prisoners; however, when routines are not followed or are changed/disrupted, this can be extremely challenging. This issue is potentially compounded by a lack of information on such disruptions. Additionally, rules which restrict the often highly focused interests of autistic prisoners can be distressing, particularly if they are part of coping strategies for other challenges in custody. Sensory challenges, particularly loud and inescapable noise, can be very distressing for autistic prisoners. Additionally, light, smell and touch (particularly use of restraints) can lead to challenging situations. In responding, prison staff may be faced with what the authors term an 'iceberg'—that is, outwardly observable behaviours designed to cope, which are misinterpreted, and with a hidden internal experience explaining those behaviours. All of the above can affect an autistic prisoner's readiness for and engagement with rehabilitative interventions. The authors assert that poorer well-being, caused by failure to manage the aforementioned challenges, are likely to impede engagement. The authors conclude by recommending that enhanced autism training and awareness (informed by lived experience) is needed throughout the prison estate, suggesting it is arguably one of the most fundamental priorities. Additionally, they suggest steps to address communication between officers and prisoners, challenging assumptions, adapting language and adjusting the physical environment where possible.

Themes

There are a number of clear and consistent themes that emerge from these chapters. All highlight the significant potential for autistic individuals to be vulnerable in the context of criminal justice processes and for this vulnerability to significantly disadvantage them. Moreover, all of the chapters emphasise the significant risk that this potential vulnerability will not be recognised and, therefore, that there will be inadequate adaptation of engagement with autistic individuals. A common link between the chapters' analyses is the apparent gap in understanding and perception between criminal justice professionals and autistic service users (in this case, those accused and convicted of offences). Reasons for this gap are explored in the chapters. At a fundamental level, prominent explanations for the risk of underrecognition and subsequent disadvantage for autistic individuals are the current inadequate knowledge and awareness of criminal justice professionals of what autism is and how it may present, and the limited evidence of widespread and robust training and professional development to overcome this deficit. In short, criminal justice professionals—on the whole—are simply not aware or knowledgeable enough of the implications for autistic individuals drawn into the CJS or how to respond to this.

The pockets of good practice referred to across all chapters suggest that a tailored, evidence-led and thoughtful approach to autistic service users is crucial to engagement that is both effective in criminal justice terms and not unduly stressful for autistic individuals. As such, a common theme in all chapters is identifying what good practice is or could look like; recommending strategies, techniques, considerations and adjustments which should be considered by CJS agencies seeking to enhance practice; and CJS professionals working directly with autistic individuals. One particularly strong theme is the importance of drawing on external support and expertise—including family members of autistic individuals—to achieve effective and fair experiences and outcomes. Taken as a whole, a coherent and consistent message is that there is clearly a challenge in balancing the needs of the CJS—including systemic imperatives such as protecting the public—with the specific and often complex needs of autistic individuals. However, an equally clear theme is the urgent requirement that the CJS adopt a more specialised, evidence-led, empathetic and context-sensitive view of autistic individuals in order that all stages improve in both recognising and managing their potential vulnerability, as well as ensuring that criminal justice imperatives are effectively met in the short and long term.

Ongoing Developments

As suggested in the introduction to this collection—and at various points throughout—the area of autism and criminal justice is highly contemporary, primarily in the context of the increased attention paid to neurodivergence in the CJS. Recent years have seen unprecedented levels of activity and engagement in policy-making and, increasingly, legal practitioner circles. This was kick-started in late 2020 by two key events: the publication the white paper, 'A Smarter Approach to Sentencing' (MoJ, 2020); and the announcement of the Criminal Justice Joint Inspection review of evidence on neurodiversity and criminal justice by then Secretary of State for Justice Robert Buckland (CJJI, 2021). Together, they catalysed a significant shift in policy focus across government departments, various branches of the civil service and at practice level. The CJJI has been particularly impactful, providing a range of evidence from across the CJS, with a significant proportion of this related to the experience and treatment of autistic individuals at all stages of the system. Ultimately, the CJJI made six recommendations which, at the time of writing, continue to exert influence on policy-making and practice. The recommendations are:

- 'A coordinated and cross-government approach' including a national neurodiversity strategy developed alongside those with lived experience
- 'A common screening tool for universal use within the criminal justice system'
- Systematic data collection to better determine prevalence and inform service planning
- 'A programme of awareness-raising and specialist training should be developed and delivered to staff working within criminal justice services'
- 'Adjustments to meet the needs of those with neurodivergent conditions'
- Coordinated working between CJS agencies, and other statutory and third-sector organisations

In its June 2022 response, the UK Ministry of Justice published its action plan on neurodivergence in the CJS, including how to address the identified issues affecting autistic individuals (MoJ, 2022). All but one of the preceding recommendations were 'partly agreed' to, with key areas of disagreement being the feasibility of a national neurodivergence strategy, whether to adopt a single screening tool across the CJS, the need to map out awareness and training needs prior to developing a programme, and the inability to adjust some physical environments for neurodivergent individuals. The action plan set out a number of actions to be undertaken by various agencies to make progress on these recommendations, including a 'National Neurodiversity Training Toolkit' (MoJ, 2022), with initial reporting on this to take place in late 2022 (not yet published at the time of writing). As such, it is not possible to comment yet on how much of this action plan has been implemented. Notwithstanding this, it is possible to highlight a number of developments that have occurred in recent years (both co-occurring with and as a result of the action plan) of relevance to autistic individuals accused or convicted of crimes.

Judicial figures now have more information and guidance on how to both manage the needs of autistic individuals during court proceedings and fairly determining sentence. Since October 2020, sentencing guidelines have been in force which relate to 'offenders with mental disorders, developmental disorders, or neurological impairments' (Sentencing Council, 2020). This includes an overview of autism for the judiciary, as well as cautionary guidance on making assumptions, particularly in light of variable presentation; the role of stigma; and co-occurrence of other conditions or disorders (Sentencing Council, 2020). Additionally, the latest edition of the *Equal Treatment Bench Book*—designed to assist judges in treating people fairly during the court process—contains a section dedicated to autism, including the challenges that may arise for autistic participants and potential reasonable adjustments (Judicial College, 2021). These are particularly important developments in light of research from various jurisdictions suggesting that a defendant's autism may negatively impact sentencing decisions (Allely & Cooper, 2017; Foster & Young, 2022; and for a contrary view, see Berryessa, 2018).

In the context of both police and penal custody, small but significant changes are underway to enable autistic individuals to better cope with the challenges of imprisonment. For example, in 2020, Nottinghamshire Police revealed plans for a new 'autism friendly' police custody suite, the first of its kind in England and Wales (University of Nottingham, 2020). There are currently two prisons in this jurisdiction (HM Prison Parc and HM Prison Wakefield) with specialist wings 'designed to cater for the needs of neurodivergent individuals' (MoJ, 2022), though these remain (at the time of writing) exceptions among the 141 establishments in the prison estate. More recently, The HM Prison and Probation Service (HMPPS) piloted Neurodiversity Support Managers, a new staff role initially in four prisons across England and Wales, tasked with improving 'processes to identify and support prisoners with neurodivergent needs,' raise awareness and upskill prison staff (MoJ, 2022). There have also been efforts to improve aspects of information sharing, a key problem in this area which hampers the ability to identify and support vulnerable individuals. For example, the MoJ (2022) has highlighted its Accelerator Prisons Project, which has required HMPPS to 'log ... neurodivergence within the prisoner's primary record on its management system in four pilot sites,' uniting this information with education, skills and work data, thereby 'giving easy access to a whole picture of the prisoner so that appropriate support mechanisms can be put into place.' Undoubtedly, these are encouraging developments, which give the impression of a system undertaking a slow but sure shift towards a more effective and fair approach to autistic suspects, defendants and offenders. However, it should be noted that most of the aforementioned developments represent very small steps, affecting only a small part of the CJS as a whole; and have not, at the time of writing, been subjected to independent evaluation. Clearly, much remains to be done, and one must always be wary of the potential gap that can emerge between promises of improvement and delivery.

Current Research Gaps

In addition to the significant practical change needed to better cater to the needs of autistic individuals, there is a need for a wider, more up-to-date range of research on autism within the CJS in order to fill the significant gaps in knowledge that currently exist. An excellent summary of themes in existing research, which has expanded swiftly in recent years, is offered by Cooper et al. (2022). However, they also note the importance of identifying opportunities and gaps:

> Given the size and scope of the entire criminal justice system, identifying priorities and opportunities for change is critical, and must be rooted in evidence-based findings to maximize impact and scalability.

There are numerous subjects about which we do not have any knowledge or which require more extensive study. There is limited academic literature on and empirical study of the operation of police powers in a 'street' context (as mentioned in Chapter 1), with little known, for example, about how police officers form or allay suspicion in relation to autistic individuals (Smith, 2022a; Rava, 2017; Young & Brewer, 2020). There is no specific research about how out-of-court disposals, administered by police officers, are used in relation to autistic individuals, including whether they are supported, to understand their implications. This is particularly important considering the increasing emphasis in recent years on resolution of criminal cases outside of courts.

There has been some discussion, though no empirical study undertaken, in relation to how effectively lawyers represent autistic clients during the various aspects of the CJS (see Allely & Cooper, 2017; Smith, 2022b), for example, whether defence lawyers are adequately equipped to understand autistic defendants and advocate for them before a court. We know little about the interaction between autism and decisions to grant bail or remand in custody. For example, we might ask whether misunderstanding of autistic presentation might inappropriately influence police officers and courts in determining whether accused persons pose a risk under the Bail Act 1976, and therefore need to be detained. There is also only indirect knowledge as to the use and effectiveness of special measures for autistic defendants in criminal courts, and little extant research relating to autistic individuals' re-entry into society after imprisonment or their experience of community sentences (Cooper et al., 2022). In relation to all the aforementioned topics, there is only anecdotal information, rather than empirical data, about whether legal professionals and practitioners are themselves autistic—something which could clearly influence both the approach to and understanding of autistic service users, as well as future policy development. Crucially, there are also very few studies of intersectional challenges, that is, unique issues faced by autistic individuals who are also vulnerable due to some other characteristic, such as gender or ethnicity (sometimes referred to as 'multiple disadvantage'; MHCLG, 2020). For example, there are (at the time of writing) no studies examining the differential experience of criminalised individuals who are both autistic and from a minority community (for more on this gap, see Revolving Doors, 2022).

The current levels of academic, practice and policy-level interest in autism in the CJS—and neurodivergence generally—are significant and promising. As such, one can be hopeful that headway will have been made towards addressing these gaps in the coming years.

Key Recommendations

To conclude, this section will highlight some recommendations which appear crucial to successful reform and progress in the area of autism and criminal justice. These are based on both the expert contributions in this collection and the wider body of literature in this area. Whilst many more could be included (and dissected in depth), this section will simply emphasise some of the most fundamental ones that emerge.

- *Training*: All of the chapters, and the literature generally, highlight the significant deficit in training, knowledge and awareness across all stages of the CJS. With the exception of pockets of excellence and individuals with personal experience of autism, the evidence suggests that training for CJS professionals is currently limited in frequency and quality, and is not necessarily appropriately designed, delivered or tailored. Without effective training—and the consequential knowledge and understanding of autism—it seems optimistic to expect meaningful changes in practice. At a deeper level, professional cultures within the CJS are often entrenched and resistant to training as a way of creating change. Fundamentally though, it is imperative that professionals are given, at least, a basic understanding of the autistic experience and the potential challenges that might emerge (which should be substantially informed by those with lived experience). In the long term, an effective, mandatory framework of autism training is needed (National Autism Society, 2022), with a potential model for the police being developed by Holloway et al. (2022).
- *Screening*: The contributions in this collection make it clear that a major barrier to both understanding and responding to the challenges for autistic suspects, defendants and offenders is identification. Without identifying individuals who are autistic, it is challenging to fully understand the extent and nature of the challenges that undoubtedly exist, and to address those challenges. There is significant criticism of how the various agencies of the CJS currently record and share information, which also hampers this. Importantly, the evidence suggests that autistic individuals are missed, invisibly passing through

the CJS with potential disadvantages unaddressed. A method of dealing with this issue would be some form of 'screening,' that is, questioning individuals (usually in the form of a checklist) to identify traits that indicate they are autistic. There are numerous options for undertaking this, but the priority recommendation would be a universal, systematic and accessible screening tool for the CJS. This would undoubtedly lead to a consistent and more effective approach than currently exists.

- *Tailored adjustments*: Again, the contributions from the expert authors for this collection and the wider literature suggest that, without carefully considered adaptations to CJS processes, autistic individuals are likely to suffer disadvantages, avoidable stress and negative outcomes. Typical approaches and generic adjustments, based on stereotypical assumptions, do not appear to be effective in ameliorating the challenges discussed in this book and beyond. As such, at all stages, autistic individuals will often need specifically tailored adjustments to assist them. These will often be simple and low cost—as simple as ear defenders in police custody or allowing a comfort object in court. Flexibility and openness on the part of CJS professionals is essential to this; in addition, a willingness to listen and respond to the views of both the individual and those close to them is key to understanding what works—and what does not.

- *Research*: As implied in the previous section, there is much that we do not know about autism in the CJS. All of the aforementioned recommendations must be based on evidence-led approaches, to ensure that unmet need is identified and that any changes that are forthcoming are, in fact, appropriate. This requires more research to understand and explore the variety of issues identified in this book and the wider literature. As such, a key recommendation is to enhance the body of knowledge which must underpin reform, by expanding the scope and depth of research in this area. It is hoped that this collection makes a contribution to that mission.

Bibliography

Al-Attar, Z. (2018). Interviewing terrorism suspects and offenders with an autism spectrum disorder. *International Journal of Forensic Mental Health, 17*(4), 321–337.

Al-Attar, Z. (2020). Autism spectrum disorders and terrorism: How different features of autism can contextualise vulnerability and resilience. *Journal of Forensic Psychiatry and Psychology, 31*(6), 926–949.

Allely, C. (2015). Experiences of prison inmates with autism spectrum disorders and the knowledge and understanding of the spectrum amongst prison staff: A review. *Journal of Intellectual Disabilities and Offending Behaviour, 6*(2), 55–67.

Allely, C. (2022). *Autism spectrum disorder in the criminal justice system.* Routledge.

Allely, C., & Cooper, P. (2017). Jurors' and judges' evaluation of defendants with autism and the impact on sentencing: A systematic preferred reporting items for systematic reviews and meta-analyses (PRISMA) review of autism spectrum disorder in the courtroom. *Journal of Law and Medicine, 25*(1), 105–123.

Allely, C., & Wood, T. (2022). "Cardboard gangsters", "in crowd" and "no control": A case study of autism spectrum disorder in the prison environment. *Journal of Intellectual Disabilities and Offending Behaviour, 13*(2), 57–76.

Allen, D., Evans, C., Hider, A., Hawkins, S., Peckett, H., & Morgan, H. (2008). Offending behaviour in adults with Asperger syndrome. *Journal of Autism and Developmental Disorders, 38*(4), 748–758.

American Psychiatric Association. (2013). *Diagnostic and statistical manual of mental disorders* (5th ed.). American Psychiatric Association.

Archer, N., & Hurley, E. (2013). A justice system failing the autistic community. *Journal of Intellectual Disabilities and Offending Behaviour, 4*(1–2), 53–59.

Ashworth, S. (2016). Autism is underdiagnosed in prisoners. *BMJ, 353,* i3028.

Baron-Cohen, S., Leslie, A., & Frith, U. (1985). Does the autistic child have a theory of mind? *Cognition, 21*(1), 37–46.

Berman, J., Levine, E., Barasch, A., & Small, D. (2015). The braggart's dilemma: On the social rewards and penalties of advertising prosocial behavior. *Journal of Marketing Research, 52*(1), 90–104.

Berryessa, C. (2014). Judiciary views on criminal behaviour and intention of offenders with high-functioning autism. *Journal of Intellectual Disabilities and Offending Behaviour, 5*(2), 97–106.

Berryessa, C. (2018). The effects of psychiatric and "biological" labels on lay sentencing and punishment decisions. *Journal of Experimental Psychology, 14*(2), 241–256.

Berryessa, C. (2021). Defendants with autism spectrum disorder in criminal court: A judges' toolkit. *Drexel Law Review, 13*, 841–868.

Berryessa, C. M., Milner, L. C., Garrison, N. A., & Cho, M. K. (2015). Impact of psychiatric information on potential jurors in evaluating high-functioning autism spectrum disorder (hfASD). *Journal of Mental Health Research in Intellectual Disabilities, 8*(3–4), 140–167.

Bigham, S., Boucher, J., Mayes, A., & Anns, S. (2010). Assessing recollection and familiarity in autistic spectrum disorders: Methods and findings. *Journal of Autism and Developmental Disorders, 40*(7), 878–889.

Blackshaw, A. J., Kinderman, P., Hare, D. J., & Hatton, C. (2001). Theory of mind, causal attribution and paranoia in Asperger syndrome. *Autism, 5*(2), 147–163.

Bogdashina, O. (2003). *Sensory perceptual issues in autism and Asperger syndrome: Different sensory experiences–Different perceptual worlds.* Jessica Kingsley Publishers.

Botha, M., Hanlon, J., & Williams, G. L. (2021). Does language matter? Identity-first versus person-first language use in autism research: A response to Vivanti. *Journal of Autism and Developmental Disorders, 20*, 1–9.

Bottema-Beutel, K., Kapp, S. K., Lester, J. N., Sasson, N. J., & Hand, B. N. (2021). Avoiding ableist language: Suggestions for autism researchers. *Autism in Adulthood, 3*(1), 18–29.

Boucher, J., Mayes, A., & Bigham, S. (2012). Memory in autistic spectrum disorder. *Psychological Bulletin, 138*(3), 458–496.

Bowler, D., Gardiner, J., & Gaigg, S. (2007). Factors affecting conscious awareness in the recollective experience of adults with Asperger's syndrome. *Consciousness and Cognition, 16*(1), 124–143.

Bowler, D., Gardiner, J., & Grice, S. (2000). Episodic memory and remembering in adults with Asperger syndrome. *Journal of Autism and Developmental Disorders, 30*(4), 295–304.

Bowler, D. M., Matthews, N. J., & Gardiner, J. M. (1997). Asperger's syndrome and memory: Similarity to autism but not amnesia. *Neuropsychologia, 35*(1), 65–70.

Brezing, C., Derevensky, J. L., & Potenza, M. N. (2010). Non–substance-addictive behaviors in youth: Pathological gambling and problematic Internet use. *Child and Adolescent Psychiatric Clinics of North America, 19*(3), 625–641.

British Psychological Society. (2021). Psychologists as expert witnesses. Best practice guidelines for psychologists. https://explore.bps.org.uk/content/report-guideline/bpsrep.2021.rep157 (accessed 6 March 2023)

Brookman-Frazee, L., Baker-Ericzén, M., Stahmer, A., Mandell, D., Haine, R. A., & Hough, R. L. (2009). Involvement of youths with autism spectrum disorders or intellectual disabilities in multiple public service systems. *Journal of Mental Health Research in Intellectual Disabilities, 2*(3), 201–219.

Browning, A., & Caulfield, L. (2011). The prevalence and treatment of people with Asperger's syndrome in the criminal justice system. *Criminology and Criminal Justice, 11*(2), 165–180.

Brugha, T. S., McManus, S., Bankart, J., Scott, F., Purdon, S., Smith, J., Bebbington P, Jenkins R, & Meltzer, H. (2011). Epidemiology of autism spectrum disorders in adults in the community in England. *Archives of General Psychiatry*, *68*(5), 459–465.

Bury, S. M., Jellett, R., Spoor, J. R., & Hedley, D. (2020). "It defines who I am" or "It's something I have": What language do [autistic] Australian adults [on the autism spectrum] prefer? *Journal of Autism and Developmental Disorders*, *53*(2), 1–11.

Carthy, E., & Murphy, D. (2021). Comorbid autism spectrum disorder and antisocial personality disorder in forensic settings. *Journal of the American Academy of Psychiatry and the Law*, *49*(4), 462–469.

Cashin, A., & Newman, C. (2009). Autism in the criminal justice detention system: A review of the literature. *Journal of Forensic Nursing*, *5*(2), 70–75.

Cassidy, S., Bradley, P., Robinson, J., Allison, C., McHugh, M., & Baron-Cohen, S. (2014). Suicidal ideation and suicide plans or attempts in adults with Asperger's syndrome attending a specialist diagnostic clinic: A clinical cohort study. *Lancet Psychiatry*, *1*(2), 142–147.

Cassidy, S. A., Bradley, L., Cogger-Ward, H., Shaw, R., Bowen, E., Glod, M., Baron-Cohen, S., & Rodgers, J. (2020a). Measurement properties of the suicidal behaviour questionnaire-revised in autistic adults. *Journal of Autism and Developmental Disorders*, *50*(10), 3477–3488.

Cassidy, S. A., Robertson, A., Townsend, E., O'Connor, R. C., & Rodgers, J. (2020b). Advancing our understanding of self-harm, suicidal thoughts and behaviours in autism. *Journal of Autism and Developmental Disorders*, *50*(10), 3445–3449.

Cea, C. N. (2014). Autism and the criminal defendant. *St. John's Law Review*, *88*(2), 505–506.

Centers for Disease Control and Prevention. (2022). Autism spectrum disorder (ASD): Data and statistics on autism spectrum disorder. https://www.cdc.gov/ncbddd/autism/data.html (accessed 6 March 2023)

Chandler, R. J., Russell, A., & Maras, K. L. (2019). Compliance in autism: Self-report in action. *Autism*, *23*(4), 1005–1017.

Chaplin, E., McCarthy, J., Allely, C. S., Forrester, A., Underwood, L., Hayward, H., Sabet, J., Young, S., Mills, R., Asherson, P., & Murphy, D. (2021a). Self-harm and mental health characteristics of prisoners with elevated rates of autistic traits. *Research in Developmental Disabilities*, *114*, 103987.

Chaplin, E., McCarthy, J., & Forrester, A. (2017). Defendants with autism spectrum disorders: What is the role of court liaison and diversion? *Advances in Autism*, *3*(4), 220–228.

Chaplin, E., McCarthy, J., Marshall-Tate, K., Ali, S., Xenitidis, K., Childs, J., Harvey, D., McKinnon, I., Robinson, L., Hardy, S., Srivastava, S., Allely, C. S., Tolchard, B., & Forrester, A. (2021b). Evaluation of a liaison and diversion court mental health service for defendants with neurodevelopmental disorders. *Research in Developmental Disabilities*, *119*, 104103.

Cheely, C. A., Carpenter, L. A., Letourneau, E. J., Nicholas, J. S., Charles, J., & King, L. B. (2012). The prevalence of youth with autism spectrum disorders in the criminal justice system. *Journal of Autism and Developmental Disorders*, *42*(9), 1856–1862.

Christiansen, A., Minich, N. M., & Clark, M. (2023). Pilot survey: Police understanding of autism spectrum disorder. *Journal of Autism and Developmental Disorders, 53*(2), 738–745.

College of Policing. (2022). Mental vulnerability and illness: Authorised professional practice. Retrieved March 1, 2023, from https://www.college.police .uk/app/mental-health/mental-vulnerability-and-illness

Committee on the Rights of Persons with Disabilities. (2014). Statement on article 14 of the convention on the rights of persons with disabilities. CRPD/C/12/2, Annex IV.

Cooper, D. S., Uppal, D., Railey, K. S., Blank Wilson, A., Maras, K., Zimmerman, E., Bornman, J., & Shea, L. L. (2022). Policy gaps and opportunities: A systematic review of autism spectrum disorder and criminal justice intersections. *Autism, 26*(5), 1014–1031.

Cooper, P., & Allely, C. (2016). The curious incident of the man in the bank: Procedural fairness and a defendant with Asperger's syndrome. *Criminal Law and Justice Weekly, 180*(35), 632–634.

Cooper, P., & Allely, C. (2017). You can't judge a book by its cover: Evolving professional responsibilities, liabilities and 'judgecraft' when a party has Asperger's syndrome. *Northern Ireland Legal Quarterly, 68*(1), 35–58.

Cooper, P., Berryessa, C., & Allely, C. (2016). Understanding what the defendant with Asperger's syndrome understood: Effective Use of expert evidence to inform Judges and juries. *Criminal Law and Justice Weekly, 180*(44), 792–794.

Crane, L., & Goddard, L. (2008). Episodic and semantic autobiographical memory in adults with autism spectrum disorders. *Journal of Autism and Developmental Disorders, 38*(3), 498–506.

Crane, L., Goddard, L., & Pring, L. (2009). Sensory processing in adults with autism spectrum disorders. *Autism, 13*(3), 215–228.

Crane, L., & Maras, K. (2018). General memory abilities for autobiographical events in adults with autism spectrum disorder. In J. Johnson, G. Goodman & P. Mundy (Eds.), *The Wiley handbook of memory, autism spectrum disorder, and the law*. Wiley Blackwell.

Crane, L., Maras, K. L., Hawken, T., Mulcahy, S., & Memon, A. (2016). Experiences of autism spectrum disorder and policing in England and Wales: Surveying police and the autism community. *Journal of Autism and Developmental Disorders, 46*(6), 2028–2041.

Crane, L., Pring, L., Jukes, K., & Goddard, L. (2012). Patterns of autobiographical memory in adults with autism spectrum disorder. *Journal of Autism and Developmental Disorders, 42*(10), 2100–2112.

Criminal Justice Joint Inspection. (2021). Neurodiversity in the criminal justice system: A review of evidence. HM inspectorate of prisons and HM inspectorate of constabulary, fire and rescue services. https://www.justiceinspectorates.gov. uk///cjji/wp-content/uploads/sites/2/2021/07/Neurodiversity-evidence-review-web-2021.pdf (accessed 6 March 2023)

Daniels, A. M., & Mandell, D. S. (2014). Explaining differences in age at autism spectrum disorder diagnosis: A critical review. *Autism, 18*(5), 583–597.

de la Cuesta, G. (2010). A selective review of offending behaviour in individuals with autism spectrum disorders. *Journal of Learning Disabilities and Offending Behaviour, 1*(2), 47–58.

Debbaudt, D. (2002). *Autism, advocates and law enforcement professionals: Recognising and reducing risk situations for people with autism spectrum disorders.* Jessica Kingsley.

Department of Health. (2009). The Bradley Report: Lord Bradley's review of people with mental health problems or learning disabilities in the criminal justice system. https://lx.iriss.org.uk/sites/default/files/resources/The%20Bradley%20 report.pdf (accessed 6 March 2023)

Department of Health and Social Care, Department for Education. (2021). *The national strategy for autistic children, young people and adults: 2021 to 2026.* HM Stationery Office.

Dickie, I., Reveley, S., & Dorrity, A. (2018). The criminal justice system and people on the autism spectrum: Perspectives on awareness and identification. *Journal of Applied Psychology and Social Sciences, 4*(1), 1–21.

Dickie, I., Reveley, S., & Dorrity, A. (2019). Adults with a diagnosis of autism: Personal experiences of engaging with regional criminal justice services. *Journal of Applied Psychology and Social Science, 4*(2), 52–70.

Enayati, J., Grann, M., Lubbe, S., & Fazel, S. (2008). Psychiatric morbidity in arsonists referred for forensic psychiatric assessment in Sweden. *Journal of Forensic Psychiatry and Psychology, 19*(2), 139–147.

Equality and Human Rights Commission. (2020). Inclusive justice: A system designed for all. https://www.equalityhumanrights.com/en/publication-download/inclusive-justice-system-designed-all (accessed 6 March 2023)

Faccini, L., & Allely, C. S. (2017). Rare instances of individuals with autism supporting or engaging in terrorism. *Journal of Intellectual Disabilities and Offending Behaviour, 8*(2), 70–82.

Falck-Ytter, T., Carlström, C., & Johansson, M. (2014). Eye contact modulates cognitive processing differently in children with autism. *Child Development, 86*(1), 37–47.

Fazio, R. L., Pietz, C. A., & Denney, R. L. (2012). An estimate of the prevalence of autism-spectrum disorders in an incarcerated population. *Open Access Journal of Forensic Psychology, 4,* 69–80.

Fenigstein, A., & Vanable, P. A. (1992). Paranoia and self-consciousness. *Journal of Personality and Social Psychology, 62*(1), 129–138.

Forrester, A., Hopkin, G., Bryant, L., Slade, K., & Samele, C. (2020). Alternatives to custodial remand for women in the criminal justice system: A multi-sector approach. *Criminal Behaviour and Mental Health, 30*(2–3), 68–78.

Foster, S. (2015). Autism is not a tragedy…ignorance is: Suppressing evidence of Asperger's syndrome and high-functioning autism in capital trials prejudices defendant's for A death sentence. *Lincoln Memorial University Law Review, 2,* 9–28.

Foster, T., & Young, R. (2022). Brief report: Sentencing outcomes for offenders on the autism spectrum. *Journal of Autism and Developmental Disorders, 52*(7), 3314–3320.

Freckelton, I. (2013). Autism spectrum disorder: Forensic issues and challenges for mental health professionals and courts. *Journal of Applied Research in Intellectual Disabilities, 26*(5), 420.

Freckelton, I. (2021). Expert evidence about autism spectrum disorder. In F. R. Volkmar, R. Loftin, A. Westphal, & M. Woodbury-Smith (Eds.), *Handbook of autism spectrum disorder and the law*. Springer.

Freckelton, I., & List, D. (2009). Asperger's disorder, criminal responsibility and criminal culpability. *Psychiatry, Psychology and Law, 16*(1), 16–40.

Gardner, L., & Campbell, J. M. (2020). Law enforcement officers: Preparation for calls involving autism: Prior experiences and response to training. *Journal of Autism and Developmental Disorders, 50*(12), 4221–4229.

Gardner, L., Campbell, J. M., & Westdal, J. (2019). Brief report: Descriptive analysis of law enforcement officers' experiences with and knowledge of autism. *Journal of Autism and Developmental Disorders, 49*(3), 1278–1283.

George, R., Crane, L., Bingham, A., Pophale, C., & Remington, A. (2018). Legal professionals' knowledge and experience of autistic adults in the family justice system. *Journal of Social Welfare and Family Law, 40*(1), 78–97.

Gerry, F. & Cooper, P. (2017). Expert evidence. In P. Cooper & H. Norton (Eds.), *Vulnerable people and the criminal justice system a guide to law and practice*. Oxford University Press.

Gerry, F. (2021). Trauma-informed courts (Pt 1). *New Law Journal, 171*(7919), 16–18.

Ghaziuddin, M., Ghaziuddin, N., & Greden, J. (2002). Depression in persons with autism: Implications for research and clinical care. *Journal of Autism and Developmental Disorders, 32*(4), 299–306.

Ghaziuddin, M., Weidmer-Mikhail, E., & Ghaziuddin, N. (1998). Comorbidity of Asperger syndrome: A preliminary report. *Journal of Intellectual Disability Research, 42*(4), 279–283.

Gibbs, V., & Haas, K. (2020). Interactions between the police and the Autistic community in Australia: Experiences and perspectives of autistic adults and parents/carers. *Journal of Autism and Developmental Disorders, 50*(12), 4513–4526.

Gillberg, C., & Billstedt, E. (2000). Autism and Asperger syndrome: Coexistence with other clinical disorders. *Acta Psychiatrica Scandinavica, 102*(5), 321–330.

Goddard, L., Howlin, P., Dritschel, B., & Patel, T. (2007). Autobiographical memory and social problem solving in Asperger's syndrome. *Journal of Autism and Developmental Disorders, 37*(2), 291–300.

Goffman, E. (1963). *Stigma*. Penguin.

Gormley, C., & Watson, N. (2021). Inaccessible justice: Exploring the barriers to justice and fairness for disabled people accused of a crime. *Howard Journal of Crime and Justice, 60*(4), 493–510.

Grant, T., Furlano, R., Hall, L., & Kelley, E. (2018). Criminal responsibility in autism spectrum disorder: A critical review examining empathy and moral reasoning. *Canadian Psychology/Psychologie Canadienne, 59*(1), 65–75.

Gudjonsson, G. (1989). Compliance in an interrogative situation: A new scale. *Personality and Individual Differences, 10*(5), 535–540.

Gudjonsson, G. (1997). *The Gudjonsson suggestibility scales manual*. Psychology Press.

Gudjonsson, G. H. (2003). *The psychology of interrogations and confessions: A handbook*. John Wiley and Sons.

Gudjonsson, G. H., Sigurdsson, J. F., Bragason, O. O., Einarsson, E., & Valdimarsdottir, E. B. (2004). Confessions and denials and the relationship with personality. *Legal and Criminological Psychology, 9*(1), 121–133.

Haas, K., & Gibbs, V. (2021). Does a person's autism play a role in their interactions with police: The perceptions of autistic adults and parent/carers. *Journal of Autism and Developmental Disorders, 51*(5), 1628–1640.

Haley, J., & Yates, R. (2020). Exploring the value of person-centred encounter groups today - Relevance, purpose and importance. *Person-Centered and Experiential Psychotherapies, 19*(3), 189–199.

Hare, D. J., Gould, J., Mills, R., & Wing, L. (1999). *A preliminary study of individuals with autistic spectrum disorders in three special hospitals in England.* National Autistic Society.

Hayley, J., & Yates, R. (2020). Exploring the value of person-centred encounter groups today-relevance purpose and importance. *Person Centred and Experiential Psychotherapies, 19*(3), 189–199.

Health Education England. (2022). The Oliver McGowan mandatory training in learning disability and autism. NHS.

Helverschou, S. B., Rasmussen, K., Steindal, K., Søndanaa, E., Nilsson, B., & Nøttestad, J. A. (2015). Offending profiles of individuals with autism spectrum disorder: A study of all individuals with autism spectrum disorder examined by the forensic psychiatric service in Norway between 2000 and 2010. *Autism, 19*(7), 850–858.

Helverschou, S. B., Steindal, K., Nøttestad, J. A., & Howlin, P. (2018). Personal experiences of the criminal justice system by individuals with autism spectrum disorders. *Autism, 22*(4), 460–468.

Hepworth, D. (2017). A critical review of current police training and policy for autism spectrum disorder. *Journal of Intellectual Disability and Offending Behaviour, 8*(4), 212–222.

Heyworth, M. (2020). Milton's double empathy problem: A summary for non-academics. Reframing autism. https://reframingautism.org.au/miltons-double-empathy-problem-a-summary-for-non-academics/ (accessed 6 March 2023)

Higgs, T., & Carter, A. J. (2015). Autism spectrum disorder and sexual offending: Responsivity in forensic interventions. *Aggression and Violent Behavior, 22,* 112–119.

HM Courts and Tribunals Service. (2022). HM courts and tribunals service engagement groups – Public user engagement groups. https://www.gov.uk/guidance/hm-courts-and-tribunals-service-engagement-groups#public-user-engagement-groups (accessed 28 February 2023)

Hollomotz, A., & Talbot, J. (2021). Designing solutions for improved support within health, social care and criminal justice for adults with learning disabilities and/or autism who have offended. *Howard Journal of Crime and Justice, 60*(2), 185–208.

Holloway, C., Munro, N., Cossburn, K., & Ropar, D. (2022). A pilot study of co-produced autism training for police custody staff: Evaluating the impact on perceived knowledge change and behaviour intentions. *Policing: An International Journal of Police Strategies and Management, 45*(3), 434–447.

House of Commons Library. (2018). Treatment of adults with autism by the criminal justice system. Debate Pack no, CDP-2018-0022, Westminster Hall 30 January.

https://commonslibrary.parliament.uk/research-briefings/cdp-2018-0022/ (accessed 6 March 2023)

Hughes, C. (2016). *Developing autism accreditation for prison services.* National Autistic Society.

Hughes, C. (2019). *Supporting autistic people in prison and probation services.* National Autistic Society.

Im, D. S. (2016a). Template to perpetrate: An update on violence in autism spectrum disorder. *Harvard Review of Psychiatry, 24*(1), 14.

Im, D. S. (2016b). Trauma as a contributor to violence in autism spectrum disorder. *Journal of the American Academy of Psychiatry and the Law, 44*(2), 184–192.

Independent Commission on Mental Health and Policing. (2013). https://www.londoncouncils.gov.uk/node/1530 (accessed 6 March 2023)

Ireland, J. L. (2012). *Summary report. Evaluating expert witness psychological reports: Exploring quality.* Family Justice Council.

Jacobsen, P. (2003). *Asperger syndrome and psychotherapy.* Kingsley.

Jarram, M. (2020). New cells for autistic prisoners to be built in £17m Radford Road custody suite. Nottinghamshire live.

Johnson, J. L., Goodman, G. S., & Mundy, P. C. (2018). Autism spectrum disorder, memory, and the legal system: Knowns and unknowns. In J. Johnson, G. Goodman, & P. Mundy (Eds.), *The Wiley handbook of memory, autism spectrum disorder, and the law.* Wiley Blackwell.

Judicial College. (2021). Equal treatment bench book (July 2022 revision). https://www.judiciary.uk/wp-content/uploads/2022/10/Equal-Treatment-Bench-Book-July-2022-revision-2.pdf (accessed 6 March 2023)

Jurek, L., Longuet, Y., Baltazar, M., Amestoy, A., Schmitt, V., Desmurget, M., & Geoffray, M. M. (2019). How did I get so late so soon? A review of time processing and management in autism. *Behavioural Brain Research, 374*, 112121.

Kapp, S. K., Steward, R., Crane, L., Elliott, D., Elphick, C., Pellicano, E., & Russell, G. (2019). 'People should be allowed to do what they like': Autistic adults' views and experiences of stimming. *Autism, 23*(7), 1782–1792.

Kenny, L., Hattersley, C., Molins, B., Buckley, C., Povey, C., & Pellicano, E. (2016). Which terms should be used to describe autism? Perspectives from the UK autism community. *Autism, 20*(4), 442–462.

King, C., & Murphy, G. H. (2014). A systematic review of people with autism spectrum disorder and the criminal justice system. *Journal of Autism and Developmental Disorders, 44*(11), 2717–2733.

Kroncke, A. P., Willard, M., & Huckabee, H. (2016). Forensic assessment for autism spectrum disorder. In A. P. Kroncke, M. Willard, & H. Huckabee (Eds.), *Assessment of autism spectrum disorder: Critical issues in clinical, forensic and school settings.* Springer.

Kumagami, T., & Matsuura, N. (2009). Prevalence of pervasive developmental disorder in juvenile court cases in Japan. *Journal of Forensic Psychiatry and Psychology, 20*(6), 974–987.

Kuusikko, S., Pollock-Wurman, R., Jussila, K., Carter, A. S., Mattila, M.-L., Ebeling, H., Pauls, D. L., & Moilanen, I. (2008). Social anxiety in high-functioning children and adolescents with autism and Asperger syndrome. *Journal of Autism and Developmental Disorders, 38*(9), 1697–1709.

Lakhani, N. (2017). Met's restraint on autistic boy "was not justified". *The Independent.* https://www.independent.co.uk/news/uk/crime/met-s-restraint-on-autistic-boy-was-not-justified-7570357.html (accessed 6 March 2023)

Lakhani, S. (2021). *Video gaming and (violent) extremism: An exploration of the current landscape, trends, and threats.* European Commission Radicalisation Awareness Network.

Lam, L. T. (2014). Internet gaming addiction, problematic use of the Internet, and sleep problems: A systematic review. *Current Psychiatry Reports, 16*(4), 444.

Lerner, M. D., Haque, O. S., Northrup, E. C., Lawer, L., & Bursztajn, H. J. (2012). Emerging perspectives on adolescents and young adults with high-functioning autism spectrum disorders, violence, and criminal law. *Journal of the American Academy of Psychiatry and the Law, 40*(2), 177–190.

Lewis, A., Foster, M., Hughes, C., & Turner, K. (2016). Improving the management of prisoners with autistic spectrum disorders (ASD). *Prison Service Journal, 226*, 22–26.

Lewis, A., Pritchett, R., Hughes, C., & Turner, K. (2015). Development and implementation of autism standards for prisons. *Journal of Intellectual Disabilities and Offending Behaviour, 6*(2), 68–80.

Lord, C., Pickles, A., McLennan, J., Rutter, M., Bregman, J., Folstein, S., Fombonne, E., Leboyer, M., Minshew, N. (1997). Diagnosing autism: Analyses of data from the autism diagnostic interview. *Journal of Autism and Developmental Disorders, 27*(5), 501–517.

Lord, C., Risi, S., Lambrecht, L., Cook, E. H., Leventhal, B. L., DiLavore, P. C., Pickles, A., & Rutter, M. (2000). The autism diagnostic observation schedule—Generic: A standard measure of social and communication deficits associated with the spectrum of autism. *Journal of Autism and Developmental Disorders, 30*(3), 205–223.

Loureiro, D., Machado, A., Silva, T., Veigas, T., Ramalheira, C., & Cerejeira, J. (2018). Higher autistic traits among criminals, but no link to psychopathy: Findings from a high-security prison in Portugal. *Journal of Autism and Developmental Disorders, 48*(9), 3010–3020.

MacMullin, J. A., Lunsky, Y., & Weiss, J. A. (2016). Plugged in: Electronics use in youth and young adults with autism spectrum disorder. *Autism, 20*(1), 45–54.

Mahbub Hossain, M., Khan, N., Sultana, A., Ma, P., McKyer, L., Uddin Ahmed, H., & Purohit, N. (2020). Prevalence of comorbid psychiatric disorders among people with autism spectrum disorder: An umbrella review of systematic reviews and meta-analyses. *Psychiatry Research, 287*, 112922.

Maister, L., Simons, J. S., & Plaisted-Grant, K. (2013). Executive functions are employed to process episodic and relational memories in children with autism spectrum disorders. *Neuropsychology, 27*(6), 615–627.

Maras, K. L., & Bowler, D. M. (2012). Brief report: Suggestibility, compliance and psychological traits in high-functioning adults with autism spectrum disorder. *Research in Autism Spectrum Disorders, 6*(3), 1168–1175.

Maras, K., Mulcahy, S., Crane, L., Hawken, T., & Memon, A. (2018). Obtaining best evidence from the autistic interviewee: Police-reported challenges, legal requirements and psychological research-based recommendations. *Investigative Interviewing: Research and Practice, 9*(1), 52–60.

Maras, K. L., Crane, L., Mulcahy, S., Hawken, T., Cooper, P., Wurtzel, D., & Memon, A. (2017). Brief report: Autism in the courtroom: Experiences of legal professionals and the autism community. *Journal of Autism and Developmental Disorders, 47*(8), 2610–2620.

Maras, K., Marshall, I., & Sands, C. (2019). Mock juror perceptions of credibility and culpability in an autistic defendant. *Journal of Autism and Developmental Disorders, 49*(3), 996–1010.

Maras, K., Memon, A., Lambrechts, A., & Bowler, D. (2013). Recall of a live and personally experienced eyewitness event by adults with autism spectrum disorder. *Journal of Autism and Developmental Disorders, 43*(8), 1798–1810.

Mazurek, M. O., & Engelhardt, C. R. (2013). Video game use in boys with autism spectrum disorder, ADHD, or typical development. *Pediatrics, 132*(2), 260–266.

Mazurek, M. O., & Wenstrup, C. (2013). Television, video game and social media use among children with ASD and typically developing siblings. *Journal of Autism and Developmental Disorders, 43*(6), 1258–1271.

McAdam, P. (2012). Knowledge and understanding of the autism spectrum amongst prison staff. *Prison Service Journal, 202*, 26–30.

McCann, J., & Peppé, S. (2003). Prosody in autism spectrum disorders: A critical review. *International Journal of Language and Communication Disorders, 38*(4), 325–350.

McCarthy, J., Chaplin, E., Hayes, S., Søndenaa, E., Chester, V., Morrissey, C., Allely, C. S., & Forrester, A. (2021). Defendants with intellectual disability and autism spectrum conditions: The perspective of clinicians working across three jurisdictions. *Psychiatry, Psychology and Law*, 1–20, 698–717.

McCarthy, J., Chaplin, E., Underwood, L., Forrester, A., Hayward, H., Sabet, J., Young, S., Asherson, P., Mills, R. and Murphy, D. (2015). Screening and diagnostic assessment of neurodevelopmental disorders in a male prison. *Journal of Intellectual Disabilities and Offending Behaviour, 6*(2), 102–111.

McCarthy, J., Underwood, L., Chaplin, E., Hayward, H., Mills, R., & Murphy, D. (2016). Screening for autism spectrum disorder in prison. *Journal of Intellectual Disability Research, 60*(7–8), 704–704.

McCarthy, J., Underwood, L. I. S. A., Hayward, H., Chaplin, E., Forrester, A., Mills, R., & Murphy, D. (2015). Autism spectrum disorder and mental health problems among prisoners. *European Psychiatry, 30*(Suppl.1), 1–1.

Mesibov, G. B., Shea, V., & Schopler, E. (2005). *The TEACCH approach to autism spectrum disorders*. Springer.

Michna, I., & Trestman, R. (2016). Correctional management and treatment of autism Spectrum Disorder. *Journal of the American Academy of Psychiatry and the Law, 44*(2), 253–258.

Milton, D. (2012). On the ontological status of autism: The 'double empathy problem'. *Disability and Society, 27*(6), 1–5.

Milton, D. (2018). *The double empathy problem*. National Autistic Society.

Milton, J., Duggan, C., Latham, A., Egan, V., & Tantam, D. (2002). Case history of co-morbid Asperger's syndrome and paraphilic behaviour. *Medicine, Science and the Law, 42*(3), 237–244.

Ministry of Housing, Communities and Local Government. (2020). *Changing futures: Changing systems to support adults experiencing multiple disadvantage.* HM Stationery Office.

Ministry of Justice. (2020). *A smarter approach to sentencing.* CP 292. HM Stationery Office.

Ministry of Justice. (2022). *A response to the criminal justice joint evidence review: Neurodiversity in the criminal justice system action plan.* HM Stationery Office.

Mitchell, P., Sheppard, E., & Cassidy, S. (2021). Autism and the double empathy problem: Implications for development and mental health. *British Journal of Developmental Psychology, 39*(1), 1–18.

Moloney, N., & Gulati, G. (2019). Autism spectrum disorder and Irish prisoners. *Irish Journal of Psychological Medicine, 39*(3), 321–323.

Mouridsen, S. E. (2012). Current status of research on autism spectrum disorders and offending. *Research in Autism Spectrum Disorders, 6*(1), 79–86.

Murphy, D. (2007). Hare psychopathy checklist revised profiles of male patients with Asperger's syndrome detained in high security psychiatric care. *Journal of Forensic Psychiatry and Psychology, 18*(1), 120–126.

Murphy, D. (2010a). Extreme violence in a man with an autistic spectrum disorder: Assessment and treatment within high-security psychiatric care. *Journal of Forensic Psychiatry and Psychology, 21*(3), 462–477.

Murphy, D. (2010b). Understanding offenders with autism-spectrum disorders: What can forensic services do? Commentary on… Asperger syndrome and criminal behaviour. *Advances in Psychiatric Treatment, 16*(1), 44–46.

Murphy, D. (2013). Risk assessment of offenders with an autism spectrum disorder. *Journal of Intellectual Disabilities and Offending Behaviour, 4*(1/2), 33–41.

Murphy, D. (2018). Interviewing individuals with an autism spectrum disorder in forensic settings. *International Journal of Forensic Mental Health, 17*(4), 310–320.

Myers, F. (2004). *On the borderline? People with learning disabilities and/or autistic spectrum disorders in secure, forensic and other specialist settings.* Scottish Executive Social Research.

Myles, B., Adreon, D., Hagen, K., Hoverstott, J., Hubbard, A., & Smith, S. (2005). *Life journey through autism: An educator's guide to Asperger's syndrome.* Organisation for Autism Research.

National Autistic Society. (2020). Criminal justice. https://www.autism.org.uk/advice-and-guidance/topics/criminal-justice/criminal-justice (accessed 6 March 2023)

National Autistic Society. (2021). Autism accreditation.

National Autistic Society. (2022). "My life could be so different": Experiences of autistic young people in the youth justice system. https://nas.chorus.thirdlight.com/link/n4bhhjjwhbxk-as0nu1/@/preview/1?o (accessed 6 March 2023)

National Police Autistic Association. (2022). Alert card schemes. https://www.npaa.org.uk/alert-card-schemes/ (accessed 6 March 2023)

National Police Chiefs' Council. (2020). Counter terrorism policing welcomes proscription of neo-Nazi group Feuerkrieg division. https://news.npcc.police.uk/releases/counter-terrorism-policing-welcomes-proscription-of-neo-nazi-group-feuerkrieg-division (accessed 6 March 2023)

Nesca, M., & Dalby, J. (2013). *Forensic interviewing in criminal court matters: A guide for clinicians.* Charles C Thomas Publishers Ltd.

Newman, C., Cashin, A., & Graham, I. (2019). Identification of service development needs for incarcerated adults with autism spectrum disorders in an Australian prison system. *International Journal of Prisoner Health, 15*(1), 24–36.

Newman, C., Cashin, A., & Waters, C. (2015). A hermeneutic phenomenological examination of the lived experience of incarceration for those with autism. *Issues in Mental Health Nursing, 36*(8), 632–640.

Newman, C. J., & Middleton, B. (2010). Any excuse for certainty: English perspectives on the defence of 'reasonable excuse'. *Journal of Criminal Law, 74*(5), 472–486.

Newman, S. S., & Ghaziuddin, M. (2008). Violent crime in Asperger syndrome: The role of psychiatric comorbidity. *Journal of Autism and Developmental Disorders, 38*(10), 1848–1852.

NHS England and NHS Improvement. (2019). *National liaison and diversion service specification 2019.* NHS.

North, A. S., Russell, A. J., & Gudjonsson, G. H. (2008). High functioning autism spectrum disorders: An investigation of psychological vulnerabilities during interrogative interview. *Journal of Forensic Psychiatry and Psychology, 19*(3), 323–334.

O'Sullivan, O. P. (2018). Autism spectrum disorder and criminal responsibility: Historical perspectives, clinical challenges and broader considerations within the criminal justice system. *Irish Journal of Psychological Medicine, 35*(4), 333–339.

Oliver, M. (1983). *Social work with disabled people.* Macmillan.

Patton, E. (2019). Autism, attributions and accommodations: Overcoming barriers and integrating a neurodiverse workforce. *Personnel Review, 48*(4), 915–934.

Payne, K. L., Maras, K., Russell, A. J., & Brosnan, M. J. (2020). Self-reported motivations for offending by autistic sexual offenders. *Autism, 24*(2), 307–320.

Posick, C., Rocque, M., & Rafter, N. (2012). More than a feeling: Integrating empathy into the study of lawmaking, lawbreaking, and reactions to lawbreaking. *International Journal of Offender Therapy and Comparative Criminology, 58*(1), 5–26.

Radley, J., & Shaherbano, Z. (2011). Asperger syndrome and arson: A case study. *Advances in Mental Health and Intellectual Disabilities, 5*(6), 32–36.

Railey, K. S., Bowers-Campbell, J. L., Love, A. M., & Campbell, J. M. (2020). Exploration of law enforcement officers' training needs and interactions with individuals with autism spectrum disorder. *Journal of Autism Development Disorder, 50*(1), 101–117.

Railey, K. S., Love, A. M., & Campbell, J. M. (2020). A scoping review of autism spectrum disorder and the criminal justice system. *Review Journal of Autism and Developmental Disorders, 8*, 1–27.

Rava, J., Shattuck, P., Rast, J., & Roux, A. (2017). The prevalence and correlates of involvement in the criminal justice system among youth on the autism spectrum. *Journal of Autism and Developmental Disorders*, *47*(2), 340–346.

Revolving Doors. (2022). Exploring the links between neurodiversity and the revolving door of crisis and crime: Policy briefing. https://revolving-doors.org.uk/publications/exploring-the-relationship-between-neurodiversity-and-the-revolving-door-of-crisis-and-crime/ (accessed 6 March 2023)

Robertson, C. E., & McGillivray, J. A. (2015). Autism behind bars: A review of the research literature and discussion of key issues. *Journal of Forensic Psychiatry and Psychology*, *26*(6), 719–736.

Robinson, L., Spencer, M. D., Thomson, L. D., Stanfield, A. C., Owens, D. G., Hall, J., & Johnstone, E. C. (2012). Evaluation of a screening instrument for autism spectrum disorders in prisoners. *PLOS ONE*, *7*(5), 1–8.

Rogers, C. (1970). *On encounter groups*. Harrow Books, Harper and Row

Rutten, A. X., Vermeiren, R. R. J. M., & Van Nieuwenhuizen, C. (2017). Autism in adult and juvenile delinquents: A literature review. *Child and Adolescent Psychiatry and Mental Health*, *11*(1), 45.

Salerno, A. C., & Schuller, R. A. (2019). A mixed-methods study of police experiences of adults with autism spectrum disorder in Canada. *International Journal of Law and Psychiatry*, *64*, 18–25.

Salerno-Ferraro, A. C., & Schuller, R. A. (2020). Perspectives from the ASD community on police interactions: Challenges and recommendations. *Research in Developmental Disabilities*, *105*, 103732.

Scragg, P., & Shah, A. (1994). Prevalence of Asperger's syndrome in a secure hospital. *British Journal of Psychiatry*, *165*(5), 679–682.

Sentencing Council. (2020). Sentencing offenders with mental disorders, developmental disorders, or neurological impairments. https://www.sentencingcouncil.org.uk/overarching-guides/magistrates-court/item/sentencing-offenders-with-mental-disorders-developmental-disorders-or-neurological-impairments/ (accessed 6 March 2023)

Singh, C. (2022). *'Friendly officers day' sparks conversation and fun during autism acceptance month*. Mich OPC.

Siponmaa, L., Kristiansson, M., Jonson, C., Nyden, A., & Gillberg, C. (2001). Juvenile and young adult mentally disordered offenders: The role of child neuropsychiatric disorders. *Journal of the American Academy of Psychiatry and the Law*, *29*(4), 420–426.

Slavny-Cross, R., Allison, C., Griffiths, S., & Baron-Cohen, S. (2022). Autism and the criminal justice system: An analysis of 93 cases. *Autism Research*. *15*(5), 904–914.

Smith, T. (2022a). Caught in the net: Police powers of investigation and the risks for autistic individuals. In E. Johnston (Ed.), *Challenges in criminal justice* (pp. 100–120). Routledge.

Smith, T. (2022b). Neurodivergence in the CJS and the role of the bar (1). *Counsel Magazine*.

Søderstrom, H., Sjødin, A. K., Carlstedt, A., & Forsman, A. (2004). Adult psychopathic personality with childhood-onset hyperactivity and conduct disorder: A central problem constellation in forensic psychiatry. *Psychiatry Research, 121*(3), 271–280.

Søndenaa, E., Helverschou, S. B., Steindal, K., Rasmussen, K., Nilson, B., & Nøttestad, J. A. (2014). Violence and sexual offending behavior in people with autism spectrum disorder who have undergone a psychiatric forensic examination. *Psychological Reports, 115*(1), 32–43.

Suttie, J. (2016). Can empathy improve policing? Greater good magazine. Retrieved March 1, 2023, from https://greatergood.berkeley.edu/article/item/can_empathy _improve_policing

Talbot, J. (2009). No one knows: Offenders with learning disabilities and learning difficulties. *International Journal of Prisoner Health, 5*(3), 141–152.

Taylor, J. K., Mesibov, D. G., & Debbaudt, D. (2009). Autism in the criminal justice system. Autism risk and safety management. https://autismriskmanagement. com/wp-content/uploads/2016/07/Autism_Criminal_Justice.pdf (accessed 6 March 2023)

Tint, A., Palucka, A. M., Bradley, E., Weiss, J. A., & Lunsky, Y. (2017). Correlates of police involvement among adolescents and adults with autism spectrum disorder. *Journal of Autism and Developmental Disorders, 47*(9), 2639–2647.

The Advocate's Gateway. (2016). Toolkit 3: Planning to question someone with an autism spectrum disorder including Asperger syndrome. https://www.theadvo-catesgateway.org/_files/ugd/1074f0_aee057da809d412f88afd683dcc402e7.pdf (accessed 6 March 2023)

The General Council of the Bar Ethics Committee. (2021). *Witness preparation.* General Council of the Bar.

Underwood, L., Forrester, A., Chaplin, E., & McCarthy, J. (2013). Prisoners with neurodevelopmental disorders. *Journal of Intellectual Disabilities and Offending Behaviour, 4*(1–2), 17–23.

Underwood, L., McCarthy, J., Chaplin, E., Forrester, A., Mills, R., & Murphy, D. (2016). Autism spectrum disorder traits among prisoners. *Advances in Autism, 2*(3), 106–117.

United Nations. (2006). *Convention on the rights of persons with disabilities.* United Nations.

United Nations. (2019). *Rights of persons with disabilities: Report of the Special rapporteur on the rights of persons with disabilities.* A/HRC/43/41.

User Voice, Queen's University Belfast. (2022). Coping with Covid in prison: The impact of the prisoner lockdown. User Voice.

Verbeke, P., Vermeulen, G., Meysman, M., & Vander Beken, T. (2015). Protecting the fair trial rights of mentally disordered defendants in criminal proceedings: Exploring the need for further EU action. *International Journal of Law and Psychiatry, 41*, 67–75.

Vermeulen, P. (2012). *Autism as context blindness.* AAPC Publishing.

Vinter, L. P. (2020). *Working with autistic individuals in prison-based interventions to address sexual offending.* PhD thesis, Nottingham Trent University, Nottingham. https://doi.org/10.1080/1068316X.2020.1781119

Vinter, L. P., Dillon, G., & Winder, B. (2020). 'People don't like you when you're different': Exploring the prison experiences of autistic individuals. *Psychology, Crime and Law*, 1–20.

Vivanti, G. (2020). Ask the editor: What is the most appropriate way to talk about individuals with a diagnosis of autism? *Journal of Autism and Developmental Disorders*, *50*(2), 691–693.

Wachtel, L. E., & Shorter, E. (2013). Autism plus psychosis: A "one-two punch" risk for tragic violence? *Medical Hypotheses*, *81*(3), 404–409.

Wallace, D. H., Tyler, J., McGee-Hassrick, D., & E. (2021). Interactions between individuals on the autism spectrum and the police: The fears of parents, caregivers, and professionals. *Policing: A Journal of Policy and Practice*, *15*(2), 950–964.

Ward, T., Day, A., Howells, K., & Birgden, A. (2004). The multifactor offender readiness model. *Aggression and Violent Behavior*, *9*(6), 645–673.

Warwickshire Police. (2020). Teen sentenced for right wing terrorism offences. https://www.warwickshire.police.uk/news/warwickshire/news/2020/november/teen-sentenced-for-right-wing-terrorism-offences/ (accessed 6 March 2023)

Weiss, J., & Fardella, M. A. (2018). Victimization and perpetration experiences of adults with autism. *Frontiers in Psychiatry*, *9*. https://doi.org/10.3389/fpsyt.2018.00203

Wilson, C. E., Roberts, G., Gillan, N., Ohlsen, C., Robertson, D., & Zinkstok, J. (2014). The NICE guideline on recognition, referral, diagnosis and management of adults on the autism spectrum. *Advances in Mental Health and Intellectual Disabilities*, *8*(1), 3–14.

Woods, R. (2017). Exploring how the social model of disability can be re-invigorated for autism: In response to Jonathan Levitt. *Disability and Society*, *32*(7), 1090–1095.

World Health Organization. (2019). *International statistical classification of diseases and related health problems* (11th ed.). https://www.who.int/standards/classifications/classification-of-diseases (accessed 6 March 2023)

Young, K. (2009). Internet addiction: Diagnosis and treatment considerations. *Journal of Contemporary Psychotherapy*, *39*(4), 241–246.

Young, R. L., & Brewer, N. (2020). Brief report: Perspective taking deficits, autism spectrum disorder, and allaying police officers' suspicions about criminal involvement. *Journal of Autism and Developmental Disorders*, *50*(6), 2234–2239.

Young, S., González, R. A., Mullens, H., Mutch, L., Malet-Lambert, I., & Gudjonsson, G. H. (2018). Neurodevelopmental disorders in prison inmates: Comorbidity and combined associations with psychiatric symptoms and behavioural disturbance. *Psychiatry Research*, *261*, 109–115.

Further Recommended Reading

Allely, C. (2022). *Autism Spectrum Disorder in the criminal justice system: A guide to understanding suspects, defendants and offenders with autism.* Routledge.

Buchan, A. (2020). *Autism and the police practical advice for officers and other first responders.* Jessica Kingsley.

Criminal Justice Joint Inspection (CJJI). (2021). *Neurodiversity in the criminal justice system: A review of evidence.* HM Inspectorate of Prisons and HM Inspectorate of Constabulary, Fire and Rescue Services.

Dubin, N. (2021). *Autism Spectrum disorder, developmental disabilities, and the criminal justice system: Breaking the cycle.* Jessica Kingsley.

Maras, K. (2022). *What to do when conducting an investigative interview with an autistic person.* Centre for Applied Autism Research.

National Autistic Society (NAS). (2022). "My life could be so different" experiences of autistic young people in the youth justice system. https://nas.chorus.thirdlight.com/link/n4bhhjjwhbxk-as0nu1/@/preview/1?o (accessed 28 February 2023)

NHS England and NHS Improvement. (2021). *Meeting the healthcare needs of adults with a learning disability and autistic adults in prison.* NHS.

Nottinghamshire Autism Police Partnership. (2020). *Autism training toolkit.* University of Nottingham.

Tyler, N., & Sheeran, A. (2022). *Working with autistic people in the criminal justice and forensic mental health systems: A handbook for practitioners.* Routledge.

For more resources on autism in the CJS, please see the Neurodivergence in Criminal Justice Network (NICJN) Resource Collection.

Index

Accelerator Prisons Project 89
adjustments to CJS processes 92
Alex Henry v R 56
American Psychiatric Association
  (APA) 2
artificial intelligence and policing 1
ASD and L&D 57
ASD individuals: and gaze avoidance
  52; and procedural rights 49; and
  unusual behaviours in courts 51
ASD training for police officers:
  benefits of 15
Asperger syndrome 35–36, 63
Asperger time 36, 51
attention deficit hyperactivity disorder
  (ADHD) 32, 42, 49, 57
autism: common features of 7,
  32; core areas of impairment
  30, 31; and criminal justice
  processes 2; definition of 2, 30;
  and developmental and forensic
  psychology 3; difference with mental
  illness and learning disability 20;
  effective recognition of 65; high-
  functioning 30; and hyperactivity 2;
  and hypo-reactivity 2; and mental
  health issues 16; mild 30; officer
  awareness of 82; and perception 23;
  and police knowledge 42, 43; and
  research 92; self-declaration of 14;
  and social communication skills 18;
  and stigmatisation 24
Autism Act 2009 3
Autism Alert Card(s) 14–15, 43

autism awareness 64–65, 91; amongst
  prison staff 70; bill of 2019 43;
  education 80; in prisons 79; training
  65, 66, 80, 86
Autism Diagnostic Interview-Revised
  (ADI-R) 57
Autism Diagnostic Observation
  Schedule-Generic (ADOS-G) 57
autism features: Asperger time 36;
  awkward expressions/behaviours
  35; compliance 33; hypersensitivity
  to noise 12; impaired social
  communication and interaction 7, 30,
  32, 36; lack of emotional expression
  34–35; lack of\reduced emotional
  expression 32; memory impairments
  32; RBRIs 37; reliance on feelings
  of familiarity 32; social anxiety 34;
  unusual ways of speaking 37
autism identification in prisons 64,
  66, 79
autism prevalence in prisons 63
autism screening in English and Welsh
  prisons 64
Autism Spectrum Condition (ASC)
  2; *see also* Autism Spectrum
  Disorder(s)
Autism Spectrum Disorder(s) (ASD(s))
  2, 15, 62; and acts of terrorism 53;
  behavioural characteristics of 52;
  and comorbidities 59; and complicity
  crimes 8; in the courtroom 47; in
  courtrooms 7; definition of 46;
  features of 49, 50, 53, 56, 60;

high-functioning 48; as neurological disorder 24; and the right to fair trial 47, 48; and risk of radicalisation 53
Autism Spectrum Quotient (AQ-10) 57
autism terminology: identity-first language 5; person-first approach 62n1; person-first language 5, 46
autism training 91; for LEOs 17; for officers 6, 10; for police officers 6, 11, 28, 82; and police officers 43; in prisons 79
autistic behaviour and police response 13
autistic defendants: and adjustments in court procedures 61; in criminal courts 84; and fair-trial rights 84
autistic individuals: and ability to recall events 33; and adjustments to police interviews 44; and arrest rates 31; and challenges in prisons 62, 67; common features of 83; and contact rates with CJS 31; and crime rates 31; criminal challenges 5; custodial/investigative interviews 29; delievery of services to 11; and encounter groups 26; and forensic interview checklist 38; and hospital settings 64; and interaction with CJS 2; and intersubjective resonance 34; and levels of compliance 33; and mental processing speed 51; and officer perceptions 82; and perception of time 33; perceptions of 24; and police interviews 7; and police sirens 13; and prison life 63; and prison routines 70, 71; and rate of crime 30; and screening and identification 91–92; and sensory demands 3; and stereotyping and stigmatisation 14; strengths and weaknesses 30; and their specific needs 21; and time of arrest 10; and understading of language 36; and use of language 2
autistic presentation 84, 90
autistic prisoners: and adjustments to prisons 76; alienation of 68; and aversive sensory experiences 75; bullying of 68; and challenges of communication 69; and challenges of social interaction 69; challenging prison experiences 80;

and communication adjustments 80; and communication and social interactions 67, 68; and noise in prisons 74; and physical environment adjustments 80; and prison adjustments 80; and prison life 79; and prison life challenges 85, 86; prison-based rehabilitation for 76; and rehabilitation 79; and rehabilitative interventions 77; and sensory environment 73; social isolation of 68; and uncertainty 72
autistic suspects: and police interview techniques 12; and police interviews 83
autistic traits: and fair trial rights 84; and structured prison environments 65

Bail Act 1976 90
Bradley report 11

CJJI recommendations 87; adjustments to CJS 88, 89; common screening tool 88; coordination between CJS components 88; cross-government approach 88; staff training 88; systematic data collection 88
context blindness 14–15, 82
Continuing Professional Development (CPD) 27
Court and Tribunals Service (HMCTS) 21
Court of Appeal 36, 54, 56
Criminal Justice Joint Inspection (CJJI) 4, 20, 64, 87
criminal justice system (CJS) 1–2, 10, 12, 27, 46–47, 60–61, 67, 84–85
criminal justice system issues: backlog of cases 1; ballooning remand population 1; legal aid remuneration 1; long-term solitary confinement 1; squeezed funding 1

Department of Health and Social Care (DHSC) 11, 20
Diagnostic and Statistical Manual of Mental Disorders Fifth Edition (DSM-5) 30, 46
double empathy 6, 10–11, 23, 25, 27
double empathy problem 6, 11, 22–23, 28, 69, 82
double empathy theory 24

empathy: between autistic and non-autistic individuals 27; and confidence in policing 22; divide 7, 11, 23, 82; and juvenile delinquency 22; and perception training 22; training 22; and training of police officers 11
encounter groups 7, 11, 25–26, 28, 83
Equal Treatment Bench Book (by the Judiciary) 88
Equality and Human Rights Commission (EHRC) 3
externalising behaviours 31

forensic interview checklist: neurodevelopmental disorder 41, 42; personal safety 38; psychiatric comorbidity 41, 42; reciprocal communication and cognitive style 40; sensory issues 38, 39
forensic interviews: efficacy of 30; interviewer checklist 40, 41; issues affecting 30; question

guidelines 41
good autism practice 11
Gudjonsson Compliance Scale (GCS) 34
Gudjonsson Suggestibility Scale 2 (GSS-2) 34

Health and Care Act (2022) 11
Health Education England (HEE) 16
high compliance and manipulation/coersion 34
high-functioning autism 34, 48–49
HM Prison (HMP) 89
HM Prison and Probation Service (HMPPS) 89
HM Youth Offender Institute Feltham 66
Human Rights Act 1998 48
hypersensitivity 73
hyposensitivity 73

impaired theory of mind (ToM) 23, 34
Independent Commission on Mental Health and Policing 11
individuals with ASD(s): and assessment of others' conduct 54; and core deficits 58; and criminal

justice system 46; and presenting symptoms 58; and recidivism 61; and remembering\recollecting 52; and selfincrimination 55; and social communication impairments 52
individuals with autism *see* autistic individuals
intellectual disability (ID) 46, 57
International Classification of Diseases and Related Health Problems Eleventh Revision (ICD-11) 46
investigative interviewers guidelines 83, 84
investigative interviews and sensory overload 29

lack of empathy and CJS outcomes 27
law enforcement officer(s) (LEO(s)) 16
Liaison and Diversion (L&D): models 60; services 8, 47, 57, 59–61, 85; staff 14

Mental Health Act 1983 19
Mental Health Mental Vulnerability and Illness (official police guidance) 18
mentally vulnerable individuals 20
mild: Asperger's condition 49; autism 48
models of autism: medical 85; social 85
multifactor offender readiness model (MORM) 77; external readiness conditions *78*; internal readiness conditions *78*; program engagement *78*; program performance *78*

NAS autism accreditation 65–67, 79
NAS autism accreditation levels: accredited 65; advanced 65; aspiring 65; prison-specific 66
national autism strategy 4, 20, 21
National Autistic Society (NAS) 2, 14, 43, 65
National Decision Model (NDM) 19
National Institute for Health and Care Excellence (NICE) 57
neurodevelopmental differences 20
neurodevelopmental disorder (NDD) 2, 30, 57
neuro-disability 19–20
neurodivergence 20, 70, 84, 87–89

neurodiversity 20, 28, 87–88; in
    the CJS 47; and criminal justice
    system 3
Neurodiversity Support Managers 89
neuro-typical (NT) individual(s) 23

offending behaviour programmes
    (OBP) 77, 79
offending contexts 53
outcome measures (prison
    accreditation) 66

PACE (Police and Criminal Evidence)
    C Codes of Conduct 27
Paranoia Scale 34
Paul Dunleavy v R *[2021] EWCA Crim
    39* 54–55
people with disabilities: and
    deprivation of liberty 45; and human
    rights violations 45
perspective-taking and autistic
    individuals 35
police officer training and empathy 6
police powers and street policing 90
prison staff training on autism 85
prison-based interventions 79
processing time 36, 84
program performance in MORM:
    change in Criminogenic needs *78*

repetitive behaviours and restricted
    interests (RBRIs) 30, 37, 46, 83

screening tools for CJS 92
self-soothing behaviours 76

sensory avoidance 76
sensory-seeking behaviors 76
Smarter Approach to Sentencing (MoJ
    whitepaper) 87
social model view and ASD 62
'street' policing and autistic suspects 82
Sultan v R ([2008] EWCA Crim 6)
    35, 49

target factors in MORM: attendance
    78; attrition *78*; participation *78*;
    therapeutic alliance *78*
Terrorism Act of 2000 54
Terrorism Act of 2006 54
themes in autism and CJS: good
    practices in CJS 87; perception
    of individuals with autism 86;
    underrecognition of individuals
    with autism 86; vulnerability of
    individuals with autism 86
theory of mind (ToM) 10, 34, 50,
    55–56
Treatment and Education of Autistic
    and related Communication-
    handicapped Children (TEACCH) 74

UK Ministry of Justice (MoJ) 88
United Nations Special Rapporteur on
    Disability 45

vulnerable individuals' access to
    justice 1

Youth Justice and Criminal Evidence
    Act (YJCEA) 1999 52

For Product Safety Concerns and Information please contact our EU
representative GPSR@taylorandfrancis.com
Taylor & Francis Verlag GmbH, Kaufingerstraße 24, 80331 München, Germany